HISTORY NOTES

James L. Halverson
Judson College

A STUDY GUIDE TO ACCOMPANY

THE HERITAGE OF WORLD CIVILIZATIONS

VOLUME TWO: SINCE 1500

TEACHING AND LEARNING CLASSROOM EDITION
BRIEF SECOND EDITION

Albert M. Craig

William A. Graham

Donald Kagan

Steven Ozment

Frank M. Turner

Upper Saddle River, New Jersey 07458

© 2005 by PEARSON EDUCATION, INC.
Upper Saddle River, New Jersey 07458

All rights reserved

10 9 8 7 6 5 4 3 2 1

ISBN 0-13-191574-6

Printed in the United States of America

TABLE OF CONTENTS

CHAPTER 15 - EUROPE TO THE EARLY 1500s: REVIVAL, DECLINE, AND RENAISSANCE	101
CHAPTER 16 - THE AGE OF REFORMATION AND RELIGIOUS WARS	109
CHAPTER 17 - AFRICA (ca. 1000-1800)	117
CHAPTER 18 - CONQUEST AND EXPLOITATION: THE DEVELOPMENT OF THE TRANSATLANTIC ECONOMY	124
CHAPTER 19 – EAST ASIA IN THE LATE TRADITIONAL ERA	131
CHAPTER 20 - EUROPEAN STATE BUILDING AND WORLDWIDE CONFLICT	139
CHAPTER 21 - EUROPEAN SOCIETY UNDER THE OLD REGIME	145
CHAPTER 22 - THE LAST GREAT ISLAMIC EMPIRES (1500-1800)	151
CHAPTER 23 - THE AGE OF EUROPEAN ENLIGHTENMENT	158
CHAPTER 24 - REVOLUTIONS IN THE TRANSATLANTIC WORLD	165
CHAPTER 25 - POLITICAL CONSOLIDATION IN NINETEENTH-CENTURY EUROPE AND NORTH AMERICA, 1815-1880	173
CHAPTER 26 - NORTHERN TRANSATLANTIC ECONOMY AND SOCIETY, 1815-1914	181
CHAPTER 27 - LATIN AMERICA: FROM INDEPENDENCE TO THE 1940S	187
CHAPTER 28 - INDIA, THE ISLAMIC HEARTLANDS, AND AFRICA: THE ENCOUNTER WITH THE MODERN WEST (1800-1945)	196
CHAPTER 29 - MODERN EAST ASIA	204
CHAPTER 30 - IMPERIALISM AND WORLD WAR I	211
CHAPTER 31 - DEPRESSION, EUROPEAN DICTATORS, AND THE AMERICAN NEW DEAL	219
CHAPTER 32 - WORLD WAR II	225
CHAPTER 33 - THE WEST SINCE WORLD WAR II	231
CHAPTER 34 - EAST ASIA: THE RECENT DECADES	239
CHAPTER 35 - THE EMERGING NATIONS OF AFRICA, ASIA AND LATIN AMERICA SINCE 1945	246
LECTURE COMPANION	252

Chapter Fifteen
Europe to the Early 1500s:
Revival, Decline, and Renaissance

Practice test

1. The High Middle Ages (1000-1300)
    a. mark a period of intellectual flowering and synthesis
    b. saw the borders of Western Europe largely secured against foreign invaders
    c. saw a revolution in agriculture that increased both food supplies and population
    d. all of the above

2. Which of the following was a reform instituted by Pope Gregory VII?
    a. the condemnation of abbots who held political office
    b. the prevention of lay investiture of clergy
    c. the rejection of excommunication as a weapon of the church
    d. both a and b

3. The Concordat of Worms in 1122 required that
    a. the emperor formally renounce his power to invest bishops with the ring and staff of office
    b. the emperor give up the right to nominate or veto a candidate for bishop
    c. the pope invest bishops with fiefs
    d. none of the above

4. The early Crusades were
    a. undertaken for patently mercenary as well as religious motives
    b. successful in controlling the Holy Land politically and militarily
    c. to a very high degree inspired by genuine religious piety
    d. undertaken to destroy the Byzantine power in the region

5. One of the most important developments in medieval civilization between 1100 and 1300 was
    a. the victory of the Crusaders over the Infidel
    b. the dominance of vassals over their former lords
    c. the lasting victory of church over state
    d. revival of trade and growth of towns

6. The university of Bologna was distinguished as the
    a. main training center for government bureaucrats
    b. center for the revival of Roman law
    c. center for church-sanctioned spiritual studies
    d. originator of the college system

7. The underlying cause for the Hundred Years' War between France and England was the
    a. fact that the French king was a vassal of the English king
    b. French support of the Burgundians
    c. decades of prejudice and animosity between the French and English people
    d. all of the above

8. The lord of a manor had the right to subject his tenets to exactions known as
    a. *corvees*
    b. *banalities*
    c. *fides*
    d. *coloni*

9. Joan of Arc gave the French people and armies
    a. an alliance with Flanders
    b. the support of the church and papal financial contributions
    c. a legitimate heir to the throne of France
    d. a sense of national identity

10. Although the Hundred Years' War devastated France, it
    a. resulted in the transfer of English culture throughout France
    b. hastened the transition in France to a feudal monarchy
    c. awakened the giant of French nationalism
    d. resulted in lasting trade contacts with England

11. The Black Death
    a. was preceded by years of famine that weakened the populace
    b. followed the trade routes into Europe from England
    c. devastated primarily the rural population of Europe
    d. was preceded by a gradual decline in population

12. Among the social and economic consequences of the plague were a
    a. shrunken labor supply
    b. rise in agricultural prices
    c. decline in the price of luxury and manufactured goods
    d. all of the above

13. After the humiliation of Pope Boniface VIII at the hands of agents of Philip IV,
    a. the Holy Roman Empire was dissolved
    b. the popes retreated to Avignon for sanctuary
    c. vassals of the English king invaded France in support of the pope
    d. never again did popes so seriously threaten kings and emperors

14. Which of the following is in the correct chronological order?
    a. Avignon papacy, Conciliar Movement, Great Schism
    b. Avignon papacy, Great Schism, Conciliar Movement
    c. Great Schism, Avignon papacy, Conciliar Movement
    d. Conciliar Movement, Great Schism, Avignon papacy

15. Humanists were
    a. advocates of a liberal arts program of study
    b. rich merchants who either wrote poetry or painted
    c. supporters of the church
    d. scholars who looked to the present rather than the past for inspiration

16. The Cluny reformers
    a. rejected the subservience of the clergy to papal authority
    b. advocated clerical marriage
    c. rejected the subservience of the clergy to royal authority
    d. were ignored by the papacy

17. Both the Crusades and the Cluny Reform Movement
    a. show the lack of authority of the Pope over European Christians
    b. were outlets for the heightened religious zeal of the twelfth century
    c. reveal that religious zeal in the twelfth century was limited to the clergy
    d. both a and c

18. The growth of towns
    a. improved the lot of serfs
    b. worsened the lot of the serfs
    c. allowed lords to replace serfs with slaves
    d. did not affect rural serfs

19. Guilds
    a. allowed the urban elite to keep artisans and craftspeople out of government
    b. gave artisans and craftspeople a voice in urban government
    c. were aristocratic town councils
    d. both a and c

20. The method of study in medieval universities was called
    a. Humanism
    b. regula
    c. Scholasticism
    d. secular

21. The most important distinction among clergy in the High Middle Ages was between
    a. regular and secular
    b. married and celibate
    c. scholastics and humanists
    d. noble and common

22. Medieval women
    a. were barred from all trades
    b. were prominent in many trades
    c. were considered inferior by the male Christian clergy
    d. both a and b

23. The battle of Bouvines in 1214
    a. resulted in the Norman conquest of England
    b. was a major set back for the Capetian dynasty
    c. unified France around the monarchy
    d. unified England around the monarchy

24. After 1450 unified national monarchies
    a. were left in a shambles by the Black Plague and incessant warfare
    b. progressively replaced feudal government
    c. eliminated the dynastic and chivalric ideals of feudalism
    d. both b and c

25. A cornerstone of French nation building in the fifteenth century was
    a. the collapse of English holdings in France after the Hundred Years' War
    b. the defeat of Charles the Bold and the Duchy of Burgundy
    c. the defeat of Germany at the battle of Bouvines
    d. both a and b

When

1. When did Pope Gregory VII pardon Emperor Henry IV? When did Pope Urban II call the First Crusade? What do these events tell us about the role and power of the papacy at that time?

2. How long did the Crusaders hold Jerusalem?

3. Which event ended the Treaty of Lodi?

4. When were the three invasion of Italy by France?

Where

After studying Map 15-3 on page 399 of your textbook, determine the origin of the Black Death and its introduction to Europe. How fast did the disease travel? Where was it most virulent? In particular, compare the spread of the plague on this map with Map 15-1 on page 308 of your textbook. What similarities can you see, especially in Spain and France? What does this tell you about how the disease spread?

How and Why

1. What were the main reasons behind the Cluny Reform Movement? What were some of the reforms? How do you account for the success of the movement and what were some of its results?

2. What major development in western and eastern Europe encouraged the emergence of the crusading movement? What were the political, religious, and economic results of the Crusades? Which do you consider most important and why?

3. What led to the revival of trade and the growth of towns in the twelfth century? What political and social conditions were essential for a revival of trade? How did towns change medieval society?

4. Consider the Black Death. What were its causes and why did it spread so quickly throughout western Europe? Where was it most virulent? What were the results of the Black Death and how important do you think disease is in changing the course of history?

5. What was the Great Schism? How did the church become divided and how was it reunited? Why was the Conciliar Movement a set-back for the papacy?

6. How would you define "Renaissance Humanism"? In what ways was the Renaissance a break with the Middle Ages and in what ways did it owe its existence to medieval civilization?

Map Labeling

Medieval Germany and Italy were divided lands where disunity and feuding reigned for two centuries. Identify the following locations on Map 15-2 on page 311 of your textbook and place them on the map provided on the next page of this *Study Guide*.

1. Papal States
2. Italy
3. German States
4. France
5. Burgundy
6. Avignon
7. Rome
8. Aachen
9. Augsburg
10. Florence
11. Assisi

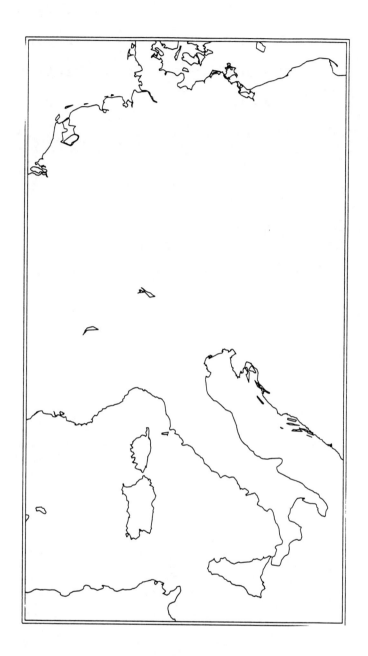

MULTIPLE CHOICE ANSWER KEY *(with page references)*

1. D (298)	11. A (312)	21. A (305)
2. B (299)	12. A (312)	22. D (306)
3. A (299)	13. D (314)	23. C (309)
4. C (300)	14. B (314)	24. B (319)
5. D (301)	15. A (315)	25. D (321)
6. B (304)	16. C (299)	
7. C (310)	17. B (299)	
8. B (306)	18. A (301)	
9. D (310)	19. B (302)	
10. C (310)	20. C (304)	

Chapter Sixteen
The Age of Reformation and Religious Wars

Practice Test

1. For Europe, the late fifteenth and the sixteenth centuries were a period of
    a. unprecedented territorial expansion
    b. ideological experimentation
    c. social engineering and political planning
    d. all of the above

2. Columbus' voyage of 1492 marked the
    a. beginning of three centuries of Spanish conquest and exploitation
    b. beginning of a process that virtually destroyed the native civilizations of America
    c. rise of Spain to a major political role in Europe
    d. all of the above

3. The flood of spices and precious metals that flowed back into Europe over new trade routes
    a. contributed to a steady rise in prices during the sixteenth century
    b. contributed to a sudden rise in prices
    c. allowed prices to fall gradually as manufacturing was increased
    d. resulted in the institution of mercantilism

4. The most famous of the northern Humanists was
    a. Francisco Jimenez de Cisneros
    b. Desiderius Erasmus
    c. Voltaire
    d. Ulrich Zwingli

5. *Utopia* by Thomas More
    a. was a theological tract that supported the Catholic church
    b. depicted an imaginary society based on reason and tolerance
    c. was an exposé of human self-deception
    d. was a simple work that supported ethical piety in imitation of Christ

6. An indulgence was
    a. a payment to obtain an office in the church
    b. a punishment meted out by the pope to heretics
    c. forgiveness given by the pope exclusively to Protestants in order to entice them back to the church
    d. none of the above

7. Which of the following was a pamphlet written by Martin Luther?
    a. *Address to the Christian Nobility of the German Nation*
    b. *The Praise of Folly*
    c. *Institutes of the Christian Religion*
    d. *Spiritual Exercises*

8. The Diet of Worms declared that
    a. the pope's spiritual authority exceeded the temporal power of the emperor
    b. the writings of Erasmus were to be placed on the *Index of Forbidden Books*
    c. Martin Luther was to be placed under the imperial ban and considered an outlaw
    d. both a and b

9. The Peasant Revolt of 1524 was
    a. successful in freeing the peasantry from feudal obligations
    b. supported by Martin Luther as a "Christian enterprise"
    c. condemned by Martin Luther as "unchristian" and crushed by German princes
    d. important in demonstrating that Luther was a social revolutionary

10. The reformation in Zurich was led by
    a. John Calvin
    b. Ulrich Zwingli
    c. Philip of Hesse
    d. Menno Simons

11. The Peace of Augsburg recognized in law what had already been established in practice:
    a. the religion of the land was determined by the Holy Roman Emperor
    b. Calvinists were to be tolerated throughout Europe
    c. Protestants everywhere must readopt old Catholic beliefs and practices
    d. the ruler of a land would determine the religion of the land

12. Calvin and his followers
    a. were motivated by a desire to transform society morally
    b. promoted a belief that only the "elect" would be saved
    c. did not depend on strict laws for governing Geneva
    d. both a and b

13. The Council of Trent (1545-1563)
    a. weakened the authority of local bishops in religious matters
    b. took steps to curtail the selling of Church offices
    c. took no steps to improve the image of parish priests
    d. changed the basic tenets of the Catholic church

14. The "King's Affair" refers to
    a. the attempt by Henry VIII to divorce Catherine of Aragon and marry Anne Boleyn
    b. Henry VIII's establishment of the Anglican church
    c. the illegitimate children fathered by Henry VIII
    d. the execution of Sir Thomas More

15. Thomas Hobbes was an important political philosopher who
    a. wrote *Treatise on Religious and Political Philosophy*
    b. argued that freedom of thought was essential to true liberty
    c. believed that people should live in a tightly controlled commonwealth
    d. both a and b

16. In what ways did the Reformation change religious life?
    a. There were more clergy than before the Reformation
    b. The clergy could marry
    c. There were more churches and religious holidays than before the Reformation
    d. Local shrines became more popular

17. Protestants stressed, as no religious movement before them,
    a. individualism and egalitarianism
    b. the sacredness of home and family
    c. the sacredness of celibacy
    d. the inequality of men and women

18. After the Council of Trent adjourned in 1563
    a. Catholics were able to peacefully coexist with Protestants
    b. many Protestants returned to Catholicism
    c. Catholics began a Jesuit-led counteroffensive against Protestants
    d. both a and b

19. The term Huguenot refers to
    a. a French Protestant
    b. a French Catholic
    c. a powerful French family
    d. the French royal family

20. The Edict of Nantes
    a. outlawed Protestantism in France
    b. assured equal treatment of Protestants and Catholics in France
    c. made Calvinist Protestantism the official religion of France
    d. assured limited rights to Protestants in Catholic France

21. A *politique*
    a. places political autonomy and well-being above religious creeds
    b. places equal emphasis on political autonomy and religious creeds
    c. believes political autonomy requires religious uniformity
    d. believes that religion has no role in politics

22. The Thirty Years' War
    a. was the last and most destructive of the wars of religion
    b. involved virtually every major European land
    c. shaped much of the map of northern Europe as we know it today
    d. did not involve Protestant estates in Germany

23. The essential foundation of the great witch hunts of the sixteenth century was
    a. the popular belief in science
    b. the strong Christian culture of rural villages
    c. the popular belief in magic
    d. d. both a and b

24. Blaise Paschal
    a. was a French playwright
    b. was a French mathematician
    c. was a follower of Calvin
    d. was the most controversial thinker of the seventeenth century

25. The most influential thinker of the seventeenth century has proved to be
    a. John Locke
    b. Baruch Spinoza
    c. Thomas Hobbes
    d. Blaise Paschal

When

1. How long after the posting of the 95 theses did the Council of Trent convene?

2. How long after the posting of the 95 theses was Lutheranism recognized at the Peace of Augsburg?

3. Place the following terms in events into correct order: Act of Supremacy, Reformation Parliament, Act of Conformity, Submission of the Clergy, Act of Succession.

Where

Using Map 16-1 on page 331 of your textbook, match the explorers to the appropriate voyage.

1. Cartier_____   a. first European to sail to India

2. Magellan_____   b. east coast of North America

3. Cabot_____   c. Newfoundland

4. Columbus_____   d. completed circumnavigation of the globe

5. Elcano_____   e. discovered the New World

6. Da Gama_____   f. died circumnavigating the globe

How and Why

1. What were the principal problems within the church that contributed to the Protestant Reformation? Why was the church unable to suppress dissent as it had earlier?

2. Was the Reformation a fundamentally religious phenomenon or a generally broader development? To what extent were economic, social, and cultural factors involved in the origins and spread of the Reformation? How can emphasis of the religious or nonreligious character of the period alter the conception of the Reformation?

3. What were the basic similarities and differences between the ideas of Luther and Zwingli? Luther and Calvin? Did the differences tend to split the Protestant ranks and thereby lessen the effectiveness of the movement?

4. What was the Counter-Reformation and what principal decisions and changes were instituted by the Council of Trent? Was the Protestant Reformation a healthy movement for the Catholic church?

5. Why did Henry VIII finally break with the Catholic church? What "new" religion did he establish and what were its basic precepts? Did this solve the problem? What new problems did his successors face as a result of Henry's move? What was Elizabeth I's settlement and how difficult was it to impose upon all of England?

6. Why was the Thirty Years' War fought? To what extent did politics determine the outcome of the war? Discuss the Treaty of Westphalia in 1648. Could matters have been resolved without war?

Map Labeling

By 1600, religious allegiance was divided among four branches of Christianity. By using Map 16-2 on page 353 of your textbook and the map provided on the next page, identify the areas dominated by the Roman Catholic Church or by one of the three largest Protestant churches, noting which church it was.

1. Lutheran
2. Calvinist
3. Anglican
4. Roman Catholic

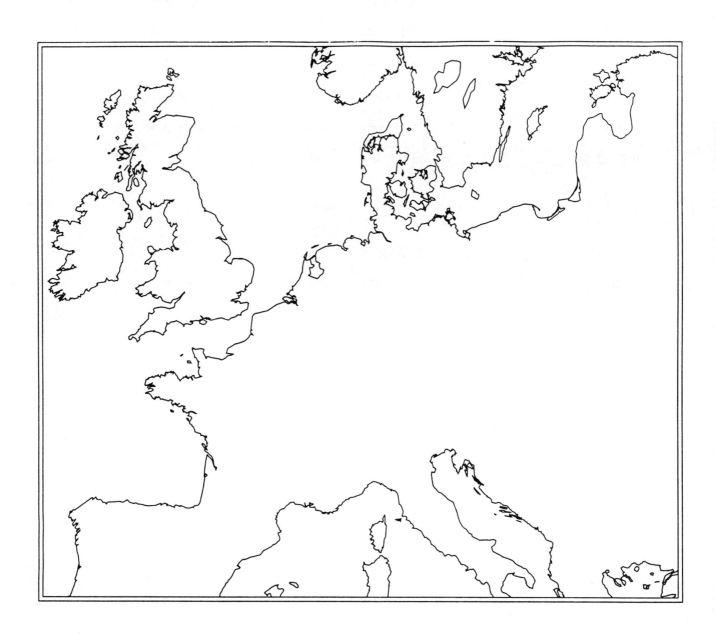

MULTIPLE CHOICE ANSWER KEY *(with page references)*

1. D (330)
2. C (332)
3. A (332)
4. B (334)
5. B (334)
6. D (335)
7. A (337)
8. C (337)
9. C (338)
10. B (338)
11. D (341)
12. D (346)
13. B (344)
14. A (341)
15. C (362)
16. B (345)
17. B (346)
18. C (348)
19. A (349)
20. D (351)
21. A (349)
22. D (354)
23. C (358)
24. B (361)
25. A (364)

Chapter Seventeen
Africa (ca. 1000-1800)

Practice Test

1. By 1800, Islamic influence in sub-Saharan Africa
    a. extended as far south as Zimbabwe
    b. eliminated indigenous idea
    c. had penetrated through all levels of society
    d. both b and c

2. After the sixteenth century, which political power controlled most of North Africa?
    a. Mamluk Empire
    b. Sharifian Empire
    c. Ottoman Empire
    d. Tunisian Empire

3. Muslim conversion in West and Central Africa was primarily due to the
    a. influence of Muslim traders
    b. breakdown of state-sponsored religion
    c. absence of hostile Berbers from the region
    d. Arabian fanatics

4. Which of the following West African rulers converted to Islam in the 1030s?
    a. Fulbe
    b. Mossi
    c. Kilwa
    d. Tripoli

5. After the conquest of North Africa by the Ottomans
    a. regionalism was crushed
    b. Morocco lost its independence
    c. regionalism persisted
    d. Egyptian power never recovered

6. Which of the following developed into a notable and long-lived kingdom in the West and Central Sudan?
    a. Ghana
    b. Mali
    c. Songhai
    d. all of the above

7. In the late twelfth century, the Ghanaian state was destroyed
    a. by Berber raiders
    b. because of the failure of overland trade routes
    c. by fanatical Almoravids
    d. by anti-Muslim Soso people

8. The greatest Keita king proved to be
    a. Sundiata
    b. Gao
    c. Mansa Musa
    d. Askia Muhammad al-Turi

9. The major source of wealth for the Songhai kingdom was the
    a. coastal trade with the south
    b. ivory trade with the east
    c. caravan trade across the Sahara to the north
    d. both a and c

10. The architect of the Kanem empire in central Sudan was
    a. Sokoto
    b. Mai Dunama Dibbalemi
    c. Maqurra
    d. Alwa

11. A significant factor in the gradual disappearance of Christianity in the Nubian region was
    a. the apparently elite character of Christianity there
    b. the eradication of its churches by hostile tribal leaders
    c. its association with the foreign Egyptian world of Coptic Christianity
    d. both a and c

12. The lasting significance of Benin lies in its
    a. court art
    b. government hierarchy
    c. political history
    d. focus on human sacrifice

13. *Trekboers* were
    a. nomadic white livestock farmers in South Africa
    b. slave traders in South Africa
    c. British governmental representatives
    d. representatives of the Dutch East India Company

14. King Alfonso I of Kongo
    a. suppressed all Christianity in his kingdom
    b. halted the slave trade in his kingdom
    c. consolidated his government and remained a Christian
    d. both and c

15. The Portuguese arrival in southeastern Africa during the first years of the sixteenth century
    a. led to the establishment of the Great Zimbabwe civilization
    b. was important for establishing Swahili control of the inland gold trade
    c. led to the establishment of the *apartheid* system that was so destructive to the region
    d. was catastrophic for the East African coastal economy

16. The mainstays of the Mali economy were
    a. agriculture and war
    b. agriculture and trade
    c. trade and war
    d. agriculture and alliances with the Portuguese

17. Arguably, the most powerful African state in the late fifteenth and early sixteenth centuries was
    a. Ghana
    b. Benin
    c. Songhai
    d. Mali

18. Idris Alawa was able to unify Kanem and Bornu through
    a. the support of Islamic culture
    b. the use of firearms
    c. the help of Turkish military instructors
    d. both b and c

19. The gradual involvement of Africa in the emerging global economic system
    a. brought unprecedented wealth to the continent
    b. paved the way for colonial domination
    c. led to a resurgence of Christianity throughout the continent
    d. both a and c

20. Trade between the Portuguese and Kongo
    a. augmented the prestige of the Kongo elite
    b. eventually centered on the slave trade
    c. led to the Christianization of Kongo
    d. both a and b

21. Swahili
    a. developed from the interaction of Bantu and Arabic speakers
    b. was replaced by Arabic as Islam spread throughout East Africa
    c. developed from the interaction of Bantu and Portuguese speakers
    d. is the Spanish and Portuguese term for Muslims

22. The decline of Swahili civilization in the sixteenth century can be attributed primarily to
    a. the arrival of the Dutch East India Company
    b. Arab dominance of the Indian Ocean trade
    c. the arrival of the Portuguese
    d. Bantu migrations

23. "Great Zimbabwe" refers to
    a. an impressive set of ruins in southeastern Africa
    b. the Portuguese name for southeastern Africa
    c. the Dutch name for southeastern Africa
    d. both a and c

24. The Omanis
    a. were a Swahili tribe who ousted the Portuguese from East Africa north of Mozambique
    b. were the eastern Arabians that ousted the Portuguese from East Africa north of Mozambique
    c. fueled a recovery of prosperity in East Africa
    d. both b and c

25. The Dutch East India Company established the Cape Colony
    a. to extract slaves from the interior for sale in the Americas
    b. as a refueling station between the Netherlands and the East Indies
    c. to more effectively support the Trekboers in their conflict with the Khoikhoi
    d. to contest Portuguese power in East Africa

When

1. Place the following Sahelian empires in chronological order: Mali, Songhai, Ghana.

2. When was the Kongo kingdom founded? How long after that was the arrival of the Portuguese?

3. According to the chronologies in this chapter, which African state survived the longest? How long did it survive?

Where

Study Map 17-1 on page 370 of your textbook and compare it with Map 17-2 on page 374. What changes have taken place from 900 to 1800 in Africa regarding trade routes and the political control of different empires? Note in particular the inset maps of the region of West Africa.

How and Why

1. What was the importance of the Ghana, Mali, and Songhai empires to world history? Why was the control of trade across the Sahara so important to these kingdoms? What was the importance of Muslim culture to these groups? Why did all of the empires fail in these regions?

2. What was the impact of the Portuguese on the east coast of Africa? Why was this European power able to gain control of certain coastal areas in this region? What was the impact on the interior of Africa because of this development?

3. Describe the political situation of northern Africa in the eighteenth century. Why did Ottoman influence decline in this region?

4. What was the "Great Zimbabwe" civilization and where did it take place? What are some of the reasons for the flowering of this civilization? What were the reasons for its demise?

5. Discuss the diversity of Cape society in South Africa. Who were the Trekboers and what was their conflict with the Khoikhoi? How was the basis for apartheid formed at this time?

Map Labeling

Identify the following regions, peoples, and states of Africa from about 1500-1800 on Map 17-2 on page 374 of your textbook and place them on the map provided on the next page.

1. Ghanaian Empire
2. Asante
3. Akan
4. Songhai
5. Hausa States
6. Kongo
7. Luba
8. Lunda
9. Ndongo
10. Shona
11. Changamire
12. Cape Colony

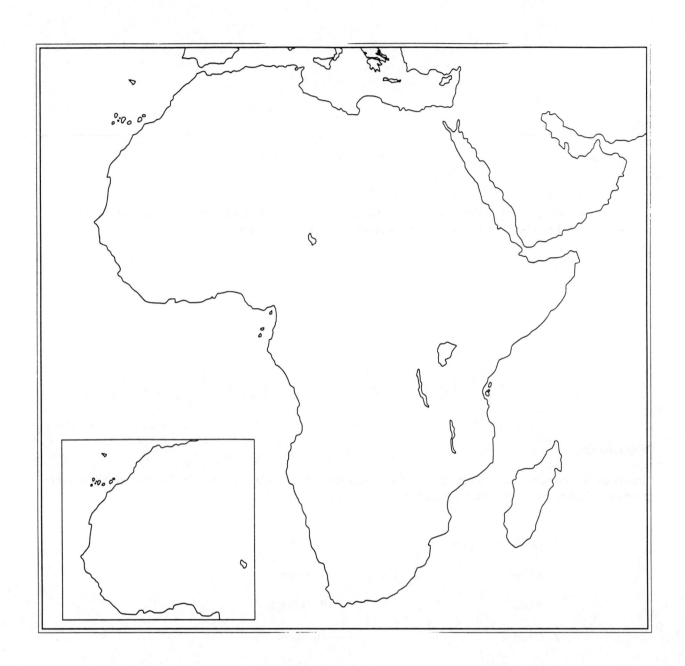

MULTIPLE CHOICE ANSWER KEY *(with page references)*

1. A (368)	11. D (376)	21. A (379)
2. C (368)	12. A (376)	22. C (379)
3. A (368)	13. A (382)	23. A (380)
4. A (368)	14. C (378)	24. D (380)
5. C (368)	15. D (380)	25. B (381)
6. D (369)	16. B (371)	
7. D (370)	17. C (373)	
8. C (373)	18. D (375)	
9. C (374)	19. B (377)	
10. B (375)	20. D (378)	

Chapter Eighteen
Conquest and Exploitation:
The Development of the Transatlantic Economy

Practice Test

1. Mercantilism
    a. encouraged free markets to increase national wealth
    b. regulated trade to increase national wealth
    c. regarded the world as an arena of unlimited wealth
    d. both a and c

2. In the New World, *audiencias* were
    a. judicial councils
    b. governors
    c. jails for smugglers
    d. religious audiences

3. In the New World, *conquistadores* were
    a. foot soldiers
    b. municipal councils
    c. local officers
    d. judicial councils

4. *Creoles* were
    a. people of mixed racial composition
    b. those born in the New World whose ancestry was European
    c. slaves from Central America who were sold in Caribbean ports
    d. those whose status improved due to reforms by Charles III

5. The African slave trade
    a. was rather narrow in its scope, directed as it was toward European markets
    b. must be seen as a part of a larger commercial system
    c. was directed to the exploitation of the New World
    d. both b and c

6. All the English colonies in North America were Protestant except
    a. Massachusetts
    b. Maryland
    c. Virginia
    d. Georgia

7. The *encomienda* was a
    a. land grant
    b. formal grant by the crown to the labor of a specific number of Native Americans for a particular time
    c. complicated system of bullion trade
    d. trading contract

8. The Spanish crown
    a. advocated the *encomienda* system
    b. voluntarily destroyed the *encomienda* system in the seventeenth century
    c. disliked the *encomienda* system because it created a powerful independent nobility in the New World
    d. both b and c

9. The Spanish monarchy received approval from Catholic church authorities for a policy of military conquest in Latin America
    a. only with strict guidelines against exploiting the native population
    b. upon signing the Treaty of Tordesillas
    c. on the grounds that conversion to Christianity justified actions of the state
    d. both a and b

10. Religious conversion of Native Americans by the Catholic church
    a. brought acceptance of European culture
    b. resulted in a very large percentage of Native Americans in the priesthood
    c. represented an attempt to destroy another part of Native American culture
    d. both a and b

11. By far the most effective and outspoken clerical critic of the Spanish conquistadors was
    a. Bartolomé de Las Casas
    b. Junipero Serra
    c. Jimenez de Cisneros
    d. none of the above

12. One of the most important forces that led to the spread of slavery in Brazil and the West Indies was the
    a. cultivation of tobacco
    b. cultivation of sugar
    c. *encomienda* system
    d. presence of small landowners in these areas

13. African slaves who were transported to the Americas
    a. generally converted to various Christian religious sects
    b. converted only to Protestantism
    c. maintained their African religions
    d. rejected their old religions and accepted the nature gods of the New World

14. The institution of slavery persisted in the Americas until the
    a. eighteenth century
    b. twentieth century
    c. nineteenth century
    d. seventeenth century

15. In Brazil, the economy was
    a. more dependent on Indian labor than in Spanish America
    b. less dependent on Indian labor than in Spanish America
    c. stable without slavery
    d. strictly regulated by the government

16. The European empires of the sixteenth through the eighteenth centuries existed primarily to
    a. enrich trade
    b. spread Christianity
    c. bring prestige to the European ruling class
    d. both a and c

17. The Roman Catholic Church in the New World
    a. was a major obstacle to Spanish and Portuguese economic interests
    b. was a conservative force protecting the interests of the Spanish authorities
    c. did not attempt to convert Native Americans
    d. sought to preserve Native American culture

18. Small military forces were able to defeat two advanced Native American cultures because of
    a. advanced weapons
    b. the susceptibility of natives to diseases like smallpox
    c. superior culture
    d. both a and b

19. In 1494, by the Treaty of Tordesillas, the pope
    a. granted Brazil to Portugal
    b. restricted slavery in the New World
    c. divided the empires of Spain and Portugal
    d. both a and c

20. The Portuguese empire in the New World differed from the Spanish in that
    a. Portugal depended more heavily on Native American labor
    b. Portugal had fewer resources to devote to its empire
    c. Portugal did not allow private persons to exploit the region
    d. Portugal did not use slaves

21. The relationship between English colonists and Native Americans can best be described as
    a. complex
    b. guided by missionary zeal
    c. disdainful
    d. violent

22. By the late seventeenth century, slavery
    a. had declined in Spanish South America
    b. increased in Spanish South America
    c. continued to prosper in Brazil and the West Indies
    d. both a and c

23. In the trans-Atlantic system, the Americas supplied
    a. manufactured goods
    b. slaves
    c. labor-intensive raw materials
    d. precious metals

24. The trade that supplied African slaves to Islamic lands is called the
    a. occidental slave trade
    b. the oriental slave trade
    c. the Arab slave trade
    d. both b and c

25. The principal carriers of the slave trade were the
    a. Spanish
    b. English
    c. Portuguese
    d. French

Where

Analyze Map 18-1 on page 391 of your textbook. What is a viceroyalty and how did Spain effectively rule its land claims in the Americas? Do you think Spain was overextended? What competitors did it face? Explain why such organization was necessary according to mercantilist theories.

How and Why

1. How did the Spanish organize their empire in the Americas? Was this an efficient operation economically?

2. What role did the Catholic Church play in the pacification of Native American civilizations?

3. Describe the *encomienda* system. How did it differ from the *repartimiento*? Why was the *hacienda* such a dominant institution in rural and agricultural life?

4. Describe the Atlantic slave trade. Where were slaves obtained and how were they treated? How did slavery affect the economy of the transatlantic trade?

5. Discuss mercantilism in theory and practice. What were its main ideas? Did they work? Which European country was most successful in establishing a mercantilist empire? Why?

6. How did the triangles of trade function among the Americas, Europe, and Africa?

Map Labeling

Study Map 18-1 on page 391 of your textbook and review page 389-393. On the map provided, shade in the areas controlled by Spain and draw the boundaries of Spanish viceroyalties. Label the areas in the New World controlled by European powers other than Spain or contested by European powers other than Spain.

MULTIPLE CHOICE ANSWER KEY *(with page references)*

1. B (386)	11. A (388)	21. A (393)
2. A (390)	12. B (393)	22. D (394)
3. A (389)	13. A (395)	23. C (394)
4. B (390)	14. C (397)	24. B (396)
5. D (395)	15. B (393)	25. C (396)
6. B (393)	16. A (386)	
7. B (390)	17. B (387)	
8. C (390)	18. D (387)	
9. C (388)	19. C (292)	
10. C (388)	20. B (392)	

Chapter Nineteen
East Asia in the Late Traditional Era

Practice Test

1. Early Ming emperors were
    a. expansionist
    b. trade-oriented
    c. isolationist
    d. foreign

2. In China and Japan, the label of "late traditional society" implies
    a. "late static society"
    b. a period of an integrated and sophisticated apparatus of government
    c. that both countries were caught in a tar pit of slow motion
    d. both a and c

3. The Ming and Ch'ing dynasties of China were
    a. homogeneous and purely Chinese
    b. both destroyed by violent revolution
    c. remarkably similar in their institutions and pattern of rule
    d. very different in terms of demographic and economic trends

4. The Ming-Ch'ing era was
    a. the longest continuous period of good government in Chinese history
    b. characterized by an absence of epidemic diseases
    c. the least prosperous in Chinese history
    d. disastrous only from a political perspective since agriculture flourished

5. In China during the Ming-Ch'ing era,
    a. the influx of silver led to inflation and commercial growth
    b. the price of land fell dramatically
    c. taxes were consolidated into one payment in silver by the Single Whip Reform
    d. both a and c

6. During the Ming-Ch'ing era, the emperor
    a. was reduced in authority and influence because of strong mandarins
    b. wielded despotic powers at court
    c. lost the support of court officials because of a breakdown of Confucian ideals
    d. none of the above

7. The gentry class was
    a. the matrix from which officials arose
    b. the local upholder of Confucian values
    c. largely urban and of the same educational and social class as magistrates
    d. all of the above

8. The Manchus
    a. were from Manchuria
    b. destroyed the Ch'ing dynasty
    c. were opposed to the Mongols
    d. worked against the Confucian order

9. The Manchus differed from the Mongols in that
    a. they despised Chinese culture
    b. they had little previous contact with Chinese culture
    c. they were already partially Sinicized
    d. both a and b

10. The last phase of Japan's medieval history
    a. saw the unleashing of internal wars and anarchy
    b. was called the Tokugawa era
    c. saw Japanese culture brilliantly transformed
    d. both b and c

11. During the Warring States period,
    a. regional lords strengthened their hold on their vassals
    b. armies became smaller in size
    c. regional lords became prey to the stronger of their own vassals
    d. important vassals were no longer awarded fiefs

12. During the Warring States period, the military class made up about
    a. 1-2% of the population
    b. 3-4% of the population
    b. 5-6% of the population
    d. 7-8% of the population

13. Portuguese exploration and involvement in East Asia was
    a. not sanctioned by the pope
    b. completely usurped by the Spanish
    c. supported by the Society of Jesus
    d. minimal at best

14. When Christianity was first introduced to Japan, it
    a. met with immediate failure
    b. was seen as a new Buddhist sect
    c. was under the leadership of the Dominican branch of the Catholic church
    d. soon resulted in a series of religious wars

15. Which of the following best represents the new urban culture of the Tokugawa era?
    a. *The Tale of Genji*
    b. a satire by Saikaku
    c. no drama
    d. a samurai painting by Sessh

16. After the unifications of 1590 and 1600, Japan's leaders sought to create
    a. a peaceful, stable, and orderly society
    b. a brutal and extractive empire
    c. a state modeled on the Ming system
    d. both a and c

17. Tokugawa Ieyasu controlled Japan
    a. by using the wives and children of daimyos as hostages
    b. by forbidding daimyo to marry without his permission
    c. by secluding Japan from the outside world
    d. all of the above

18. The political dynamism of the period from Hideyoshi through the early Tokugawa period
    a. was not matched by economic growth
    b. was matched by economic growth
    c. led to a stagnation in urban life
    d. both a and c

19. During the Tokugawa period
    a. Buddhism was eradicated
    b. folk religions were replaced by court bakufu sponsored Shintoism
    c. Buddhism became more deeply rooted
    d. both a and b

20. Which geographic feature affected Korea's history?
    a. its lack of natural borders
    b. its close proximity to China
    c. its close proximity to Japan
    d. both b and c

21. The amazing longevity of the Choson era was most directly related to
    a. the weakness of Japan during that period
    b. the preoccupation of Ming China with northern invaders
    c. the stability of the Ming dynasty
    d. the protection of European powers

22. In 1592 and 1598 Ming armies entered Korea
    a. to protect it from Japanese invasions
    b. to bring it into the Ming empire
    c. to punish it for incursions into Ming land
    d. both b and c

23. Today, Burma, Thailand, and Cambodia retain
    a. Japanese forms of Buddhism
    b. Confucian principles
    c. Indian forms of Buddhism
    d. native folk religions

24. Vietnamese rulers
    a. consistently defied Chinese power
    b. "managed" their relationship with China
    c. ruled using Chinese power
    d. looked to India to balance Chinese influence

25. The Nguyen dynasty
    a. was anti-French and anti-Christian
    b. was pro-French and pro-Christian
    c. was supported by French military power
    d. finally rejected Chinese infuence

When

1. During what period of the Ming dynasty was China expansionist?

2. When did China and Japan fight on the Korean peninsula?

3. How long after the arrival of the Portuguese was the policy of seclusion adopted in Japan? How long after the policy of seclusion was adopted did Matthew Perry arrive?

4. For how long after the arrival of the Portuguese was Christianity legal in Japan?

5. Which of the Korean states lasted the longest?

Where

Carefully study Map 19-1 on page 408 of your textbook and analyze how the rivers of China might have helped to consolidate the political authority and economic strength of the Ch'ing empire. What defensive arrangements have been made to protect against which enemies? Why was the Grand Canal important to the Ch'ing empire?

How and Why

1. How did the late imperial political system operate in China? What was the importance of education, Confucianism, and the emperors to this system of government? Compare the Chinese cyclical development with the Japanese longitudinal pattern of government.

2. How were the Manchus able to control China after 1644? How important were the emperors in the early and middle phase of Manchu rule?

3. What were the primary factors influencing the third commercial revolution in China from 1500 to 1800? What was the role of agriculture in this revolution? Why were cash crops important in this development? Where was population growth most evident?

4. Explain the main tenets of Chinese foreign policy in the Ming-Ch'ing period. What were the "managed frontiers"? Why did the Chinese fail to take advantage of their maritime technology? What groups were the greatest threat to the empire?

5. What were the main tenets of Ming-Ch'ing culture? How did the novel develop in this period? What are the similarities of culture with past Chinese dynasties? Why was Western influence of little importance in this period?

6. What were the main tenets of Japanese foreign policy from 1467 to 1858? How important was Western influence in this period? What trade had been carried on with China and why did this activity stop during this period?

Map Labeling

The Tokugawa era in Japan lasted from about 1600 to 1868. Using Map 19-2 on page 414 of your textbook, identify the following locations in Japan on the next page.

1. Edo
2. Nagoya
3. Osaka
4. Kyoto
5. Tosa
6. Choshu
7. Hizen
8. Satsuma
9. Sea of Japan
10. Korea
11. Seoul
12. Pacific Ocean

MULTIPLE CHOICE ANSWER KEY *(with page references)*

1. C (404)	11. C (411)	21. C (421)
2. B (404)	12. D (412)	22. A (422)
3. C (404)	13. C (412)	23. C (423)
4. A (404)	14. B (412)	24. B (424)
5. D (404)	15. B (418)	25. A (426)
6. B (405)	16. A (413)	
7. D (406)	17. D (414)	
8. A (407)	18. B (415)	
9. C (407)	19. C (417)	
10. A (411)	20. D (420)	

Chapter Twenty
European State Building and
Worldwide Conflict

Practice Test

1. The Petition of Right required
     a. no taxation without representation
     b. that Parliament could not declare war without consent of the king
     c. that no freemen could be imprisoned without due cause
     d. that private citizens would billet troops in their homes

2. After dissolving Parliament in 1629, Charles I did not call it again until 1640 when
     a. he was arrested by Parliamentary forces
     b. he was threatened with exile
     c. England went to war with Scotland
     d. both a and b

3. James I sought to raise money
     a. through impositions
     b. through new customs duties
     c. by asking Parliament to raise new taxes
     d. both a and b

4. From 1649 to 1660, England was officially called a(n)
     a. constitutional monarchy
     b. absolute monarchy
     c. military despotism
     d. Puritan republic led by Oliver Cromwell

5. Why did Parliament decide to accept William of Orange and Mary as successors to the deposed James II?
     a. the birth of a son to James II meant that there would be a Catholic heir to the throne
     b. James II's daughter, Mary, was a Protestant
     c. William of Orange was a Protestant leader in Europe
     d. all of the above

6. After Oliver Cromwell disbanded Parliament in 1653, he ruled under the title of
     a. Prime Minister
     b. Lord Protector
     c. Leviathan
     d. High Sovereign

7. Louis XIV's famous alleged declaration was
     a. "I am the state"
     b. "let sleeping dogs lie"
     c. "unity through power"
     d. "glory in all endeavors"

8. The Treaty of Utrecht
     a. provided an example of Spanish atrocities to British merchants in the West Indies
     b. revealed Spanish intervention in British West Indian trade
     c. was a factor in the outbreak of war between England and Spain in 1739
     d. gave Britian the right to send one ship a year to Portobello

9. France's decision to help Prussia in 1740 was a mistake because it
     a. lessened its ability to help Spain
     b. consolidated a powerful new state in Germany
     c. drew England onto Austria's side
     d. all of the above

10. Huguenots were
    a. generally supported by Louis XIV
    b. tolerated by the French Catholic church, but not by the king
    c. relocated to southern France by Louis XIV
    d. banned from government office and excluded from certain professions by Louis XIV

11. The revocation of the Edict of Nantes
    a. became the major blunder of Louis' reign
    b. opened France to invasion from Protestant forces
    c. virtually eliminated French trade with the German states
    d. led to a campaign against Jews in France

12. Upon his accession as King of England in 1714, George I
    a. was welcomed by both Scotland and Wales
    b. dismissed Parliament and called for new elections
    c. established the Hohenzollern dynasty in England
    d. was confronted with a challenge to his title from James Edward Stuart

13. The English House of Commons in the eighteenth century
    a. was dominated by wealthy nobles and property owners
    b. represented the interests of district constituents
    c. was generally responsive to public opinion
    d. both b and c

14. Who violated the Pragmatic Sanction in 1740?
    a. Leopold I   c. Frederick II
    b. Charles VI   d. Frederick William

15. Upon becoming tsar in 1682, Peter the Great was convinced that the
    a. political power of the tsar must be made secure from the *boyars* and *streltsy*
    b. military power of Russia must be increased
    c. Russian nobility must be placated
    d. both a and b

16. In the second half of the sixteenth century, monarchs sought new sources of revenue
    a. to support ever-growing bureaucracies
    b. meet the increased cost of warfare
    c. maintain overseas colonies
    d. as part of mercantilist policy

17. In both England and France
    a. there were strong traditions of the monarchy bargaining with the nobility
    b. the monarchies were able to build secure financial bases independent of the nobility
    c. the nobility stood at the top of the social hierarchy
    d. both a and c

18. Charles I might have ruled indefinitely without Parliament but for
    a. war with Scotland
    b. war with France
    c. pressure from the nobility
    d. his commitment to shared power

19. The Bill of Rights
    a. committed Parliament to support the Presbyterian church
    b. was a summary of popular and parliamentary grievances against the crown
    c. provided for the restoration of the monarchy
    d. prohibited a Roman Catholic from occupying the English throne

20. British political life
    a. was more stable than on the Continent
    b. was freer than on the Continent
    c. was more restricted than on the Continent
    d. centered on the monarch

21. After assuming power in 1661, Louis XIV
    a. preserved noble institutions
    b. abolished noble institutions
    c. ruled through a chief minister
    d. appointed powerful nobles to high positions

22. The central element of the image of the French monarchy was
    a. Louis XIV's personal charisma
    b. the army
    c. Versailles
    d. Paris

23. In his reorganization of domestic administration, Peter the Great looked to
    a. British models
    b. French models
    c. Danish models
    d. Swedish models

24. Peter the Great's desire for warm water ports
    a. gave Russia an overseas empire
    b. led to wars with the Ottomans and Sweden
    c. led to wars with Germany and Sweden
    d. led to wars with the Ottomans and Germany

25. After 1648, the power of the Holy Roman Emperor
    a. was absolute
    b. depended upon the support of a representative assembly
    c. depended on cooperation with various political bodies throughout the empire
    d. was merely symbolic

When

1. Put the following events in English history in the correct order: Act of Settlement, Petition of Right, Test Act, Great Remonstrance, Secret Treaty of Dover, Glorious Revolution.

2. Put the following events in French history in correct order: War of the Spanish Succession, Revocation of the Edict of Nantes, the Fronde, Nine Years' War, Treaty of Utrecht, War of Devolution, Treaty of Rastadt.

How and Why

1. Why did the king and Parliament come into conflict in the 1640s? What were the most important issues and who bears more responsibility for the war? What were the most important results of the English civil wars of the seventeenth century? How did England in 1700 differ from England in 1600?

2. What was the Glorious Revolution and why did it take place? What were James II's mistakes and what were the issues involved in 1688? What kind of settlement emerged from the revolution? Assess its importance for the future political history of the West.

3. Discuss the foreign policy of Great Britain under the direction of William Pitt. What was his colonial vision and how successful was he in limiting French settlement and influence in North America?

4. "Peter the Great was a rational ruler, interested in the welfare of his people." Do you agree with this statement? Why? Can you make a case for Peter as a bloody tyrant, who was concerned only in promoting his own glory?

Map Labeling

Study Map 20-1 on page 440 of your textbook. On the map provided for you on the next page trace the border of the Holy Roman Empire and use different colors or different contrasts of shading to identify Bourbon and Hapsburg territories.

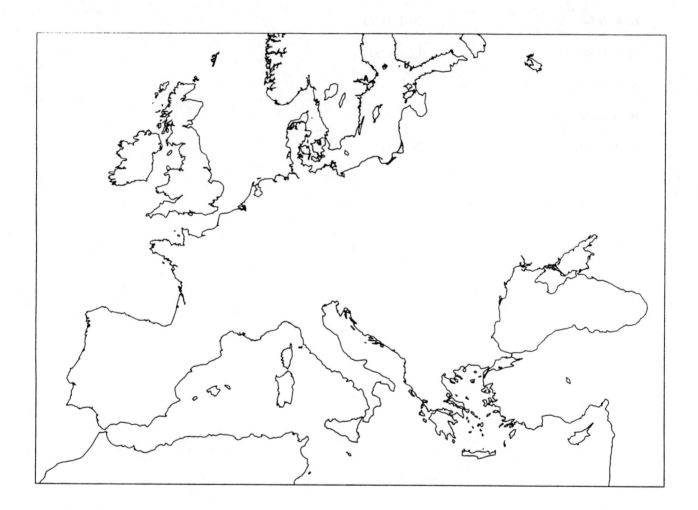

MULTIPLE CHOICE ANSWER KEY *(with page references)*

1. C (432)
2. C (432)
3. D (432)
4. D (434)
5. D (435)
6. B (434)
7. A (438)
8. D (445)
9. D (446)
10. D (439)
11. A (439)
12. D (435)
13. A (435)
14. C (443)
15. D (441)
16. B (430)
17. C (431)
18. A (433)
19. D (435)
20. B (436)
21. A (437)
22. C (437)
23. D (441)
24. B (442)
25. C (443)

Chapter Twenty-One
European Society Under the Old Regime

Practice Test

1. The invention that took cotton textile manufacturing out of the home and put it into the factory was Richard Arkwright's
    a. spinning jenny
    b. cotton gin
    c. water frame
    d. puddling process

2. The enclosure movement in early seventeenth-century Britain
    a. increased food production
    b. provided for larger agricultural units
    c. depopulated the countryside
    d. both a and b

3. More than any other single factor, what development distinguished Europe and North America from the rest of the world until the twentieth century?
    a. industrialization
    b. domestic system
    c. agricultural revolution
    d. expanded grain production

4. Those Jews who grew quite close to the rulers of different countries were called
    a. financiers
    b. "court Jews"
    c. "orthodox Jews"
    d. "ghetto fathers"

5. Socially, pre-Revolutionary Europe was based on aristocratic elites
    a. with inherited legal privileges
    b. with privileges based on military skills
    c. who controlled trade
    d. both b and c

6. Which of the following was not a chief social characteristic of the old regime?
    a. tradition
    b. hierarchy
    c. corporateness
    d. hostility

7. "Neolocalism" is a term denoting
    a. local art forms
    b. the practice of moving away from home
    c. migration from the countryside to the city
    d. none of the above

8. In preindustrial Europe, "servant" refers to someone
    a. looking after the needs of wealthy people
    b. who exchanged household duties for room, board, and wages
    c. with the social status of a serf
    d. who brought to the household a particular skill or trade

9. The agricultural revolution of the seventeenth and eighteenth centuries began in
    a. Britain
    b. the Low Countries
    c. France
    d. Poland

10. Which of the following was not a significant factor in the population explosion of the eighteenth century?
    a. the potato
    b. fewer wars and epidemics
    c. a clear decline in the death rate
    d. better medical techniques

11. How would you characterize British society in the eighteenth century?
    a. relatively mobile
    b. tightly restricted
    c. dominated by the middle class
    d. none of the above

12. The first practical engine using steam power was invented by
    a. Edmund Cartwright
    b. James Watt
    c. Thomas Newcomen
    d. John Wilkinson

13. Between 1700 and 1800, the urban population of Europe
    a. nearly doubled
    b. declined by a third
    c. tripled
    d. none of the above

14. In the middle of the eighteenth century, the rate of growth of existing large cities
    a. increased more slowly
    b. decreased radically
    c. remained the same
    d. increased only in France

15. The middle class
    a. lived in towns and were called *Junkers*
    b. consisted of bankers, traders, lawyers, and manufacturers
    c. were called the *bourgeoisie*
    d. both b and c

16. The smallest, wealthiest, and most socially responsible aristocrat resided in
    a. France
    b. Great Britain
    c. Germany
    d. Russia

17. *Hobreaux* were
    a. court aristocracs
    b. merchants
    c. provincial aristocrats
    d. peasants

18. In Prussia and Austria
    a. landlords exercised almost complete control over serfs
    b. most peasants owned land and were not serfs
    c. the condition of serfs was worse than all other countries in Europe
    d. serfs were freed from the land due to the needs of the new industrial centers

19. In northwestern Europe
    a. children remained in the household of their birth and expanded it.
    b. children left home in their early teens
    c. young people married in their early teens
    d. both ba and c

20. Household servants were typically
    a. Jews
    b. Africans
    c. socially inferior to their employer
    d. not socially inferior to their employer

21. Upon the death of the father
    a. the widow would take on the farm or business
    b. the widow would quickly remarry
    c. the family would dissolve
    d. all of the above

22. The chief concern of a married woman in the Old Regime was
    a. earning money and producing food
    b. bearing and raising children
    c. housekeeping
    d. both b and c

23. The main goal of traditional European peasant society was to
    a. become free of aristocratic domination
    b. ensure the local food supply
    c. rise into the middle class
    d. become more productive through technological innovation

24. In eastern Europe, the chief means of increasing agricultural production was
    a. employing new techniques
    b. utilize more serfs
    c. farm new land
    d. both a and c

25. Much of the history of the non-Western world since the middle of the eighteenth century to the present can be understood in terms of how
    a. it reacted to penetration by Europeans and Americans
    b. it became wealthy by supplying markets and materials for the industrial West
    c. it presented a viable economic alternative to the industrial West
    d. followed the West in rejecting tradition during the Industrial Revolution

How and Why

1. What was the "agricultural revolution" and what factors were important in its development?

2. Why did Europe's population increase in the eighteenth century and what were the effects of this population explosion?

3. What were some of the technological innovations that contributed to the birth of the Industrial Revolution? Why was Great Britain able to take the lead and benefit so dramatically from the Industrial Revolution?

4. How would you define the term "family economy" and what was its goal? What was the position of women and children within the family economy? Why was the family so vulnerable as a social and economic unit?

5. How did the British aristocracy differ from aristocrats in France, Eastern Europe, and Russia? What tensions existed between the European aristocracies and the developing middle classes?

6. What was the status of Jews in European society during the old regime? Why were they discriminated against?

MULTIPLE CHOICE ANSWER KEY *(with page references)*

1. C (464)	11. A (466)	21. D (457)
2. D (461)	12. C (465)	22. A (458)
3. A (462)	13. A (462)	23. B (460)
4. B (468)	14. A (466)	24. C (461)
5. A (452)	15. D (466)	25. A (462)
6. D (452)	16. B (453)	
7. B (456)	17. C (454)	
8. B (456)	18. A (454)	
9. B (460)	19. B (455)	
10. D (462)	20. D (456)	

Chapter Twenty-Two
The Last Great Islamic Empires
(1500-1800)

Practice Test

1. From 1450 to 1650,
   a. the ideal of a universal Muslim caliphate gave way to secular sultanates
   b. there existed a blossoming of Islamic culture and power
   c. the Muslim world went into decline
   d. both a and b

2. Which of the following empires flourished during the period 1500 to 1650?
   a. Ottoman
   b. Safavid
   c. Mughal
   d. all of the above

3. Which eventually became the Ottoman capital after 1453 to 1650?
   a. Bursa
   b. Kurdistan
   c. Istanbul
   d. Marmara

4. Süleyman the Magnificent is significant because he
   a. founded Mecca
   b. advanced Ottoman borders into Eastern Europe and the Caucasus
   c. founded Istanbul
   d. codified Islamic law

5. How did the Ottomans seek to keep their military commanders loyal to the throne?
   a. by using slave soldiers loyal only to the sultan
   b. by exiling traitors from the *ulama*
   c. through the registration and control of *timar* lands
   d. both b and c

6. In the seventeenth century, the Janissary corps
   a. became increasingly independent of imperial control
   b. resisted corruption and remained loyal to the sultan
   c. started commercial enterprises in the Balkan regions
   d. had been infiltrated by Christian zealots

7. The Janissary corps were
   a. mounted warriors
   b. the infamous slave corps that protected the sultan
   c. Ottoman administrators
   d. Safavid businessmen

8. Shah Abbas I
   a. brought a firm and able hand to the leadership of the Safavid domains
   b. was defeated by Süleyman's Ottoman forces
   c. was not popular among his troops
   d. created a provincial slave levy

9. In the long run, the most impressive aspect of Safavid times was the
   a. competent administration of foreign lands
   b. codification of Sunni spiritual texts
   c. cultural and intellectual renaissance of Iran in the sixteenth and seventeenth centuries
   d. extension of Islam into Eastern Europe

10. Among the most developed crafts in Safavid Iran was
    a. porcelain
    b. silk
    c. ivory
    d. all of the above

11. The Sikhs were
    a. a Hindu holy order of monks
    b. neither Hindu nor Muslim and had their own scripture
    c. allies of the Mughal empire
    d. none of the above

12. The greatest ruler of the Mughal empire was
    a. Shah Abbas I
    b. Süleyman the Magnificent
    c. Akbar the Great
    d. Shah Jahan

13. The founders of the Mughal dynasty were
    a. descended form Timur
    b. supported Shi'ite zealots
    c. opposed Sunni lawgivers
    d. descended from Shah Abbas

14. In the sixteenth century, Muslims began to be displaced to the west coast of India by
    a. the expanding Hapsburg empire
    b. Chinese traders
    c. Portuguese traders
    d. Shi'ite militants

15. The state of Acheh was located in
    a. northern Africa
    b. southern India
    c. northwestern Sumatra
    d. the Deccan highlands

16. One of the major social institutions of the later Ottoman Empire was the
    a. pub
    b. coffee house
    c. tea room
    d. market

17. The growing strength of the Safavids
    a. unified Iran around Shi'ite Islam
    b. brought them into conflict with the dominant Shi'ite groups in Iran
    c. was halted by the Ottomans
    d. brought them into conflict with the dominat Sunni groups in Iran

18. Guru Nanak preached
    a. devotion to the Brahmans
    b. faith and devotion to one loving and merciful God
    c. total devotion to Lord Krishna
    d. Shi'ite ideology

19. Muslim eclectic tendencies in Mughal Indai came primarily from
    a. Sunnis
    b. Shi'ites
    c. Sufis
    d. Sikhs

20. Of the Central Asian Islamic states after 1500, the most significant was
    a. that of the Chaghatay Turks
    b. the Uzbek empire
    c. Acheh
    d. Hyderabad

21. The result of the Shi'ite rift was
    a. the isolation of the Ottoman Turks
    b. a revived Chaghatay state
    c. the isolation of Central Asian Muslims
    d. both b and c

22. After the arrival of the Portuguese in the southern rim of Asia
    a. the Islamization of the area continued
    b. the Islamization of the area ended
    c. most Muslims became Christians
    d. Christianity replaced Buddhism in Southeast Asia

23. European imperialism in the southern rim of Asia
    a. was successful in spreading European culture and Christianity
    b. was successful in economic and military terms
    c. was a failure in all respects
    d. both a and b

24. The chief religious group that Muslims replaced in the southern seas were
    a. Buddhists
    b. Christians
    c. Confucians
    d. Hindus

25. The Ottoman state was organized
    a. to support Sunni Islam
    b. according to the Shari'a
    c. as one vast military institution
    d. according to European models

When

1. When did the Ottoman Empire begin giving up territory in Europe? When was Mughal India defeated by a European power?

2. Which of the Islamic empires lasted the longest?

3. Place the following events in correct order: Treaty of Karlowitz, fall of Constantinople, Rule of Selim I, Ottomans cross Dardanelles, Siege of Vienna.

Where

Using Map 22-1 on page 478 of your textbook as a guide, place the correct letter in the blank space after each term.

A. Ottoman　　　　　B. Safavid　　　　　C. Mughal

1. Delhi　　_____

2. Medina　_____

3. Tabriz　_____

4. Cairo　　_____

5. Istanbul　_____

How and Why

1. What were the main reasons for the internal decline of the Ottoman Empire?

2. What were the most important reasons for the success of the Safavid empire in Iran? What role did Islamic religion have in this development? Who were the major foes of this empire?

3. What were the most important elements that united all Islamic states? Why was there a certain lack of unity among these states from 1500 to 1800? How and why were the European powers able to promote division among these various states?

4. The Mughal conquest of India was led by Akbar "the Great." What were his main policies toward the Hindu population? Why did he succeed and his followers fail in this area? What were his main reforms of the government?

5. Why has the cultural and intellectual renaissance in Iran during the sixteenth and seventeenth centuries been called "the most impressive aspect of Safavid times"? Be specific about advances in the disciplines of painting and architecture.

Map Labeling

Carefully analyze Map 22-1 on page 478 of the textbook. On the map provided for you, identify each of the major Islamic empires, indicating the farthest extent of each empire.

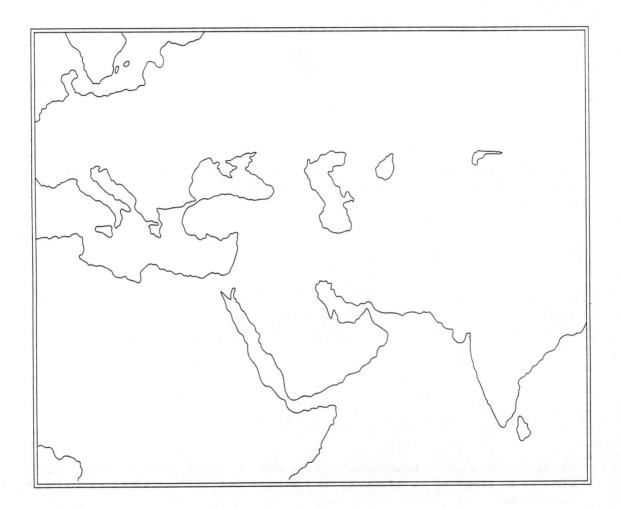

MULTIPLE CHOICE ANSWER KEY *(with page references)*

1. D (478)
2. D (478)
3. C (479)
4. B (479)
5. D (479)
6. A (480)
7. B (479)
8. A (482)
9. C (482)
10. A (482)
11. B (483)
12. C (483)
13. A (483)
14. C (487)
15. C (488)
16. B (481)
17. D (481)
18. B (485)
19. C (486)
20. A (486)
21. C (486)
22. A (487)
23. B (488)
24. D (487)
25. C (479)

Chapter Twenty-Three
The Age of European Enlightenment

Practice Test

1. As a result of the Enlightenment,
   a. the aristocracy became intellectualized
   b. distinctions between social classes were not as defined
   c. the spirit of innovation and improvement came to characterize modern European and Western society
   d. all of the above

2. The most influential of the *philosophes* was
   a. John Locke
   b. Baron de Montesquieu
   c. Voltaire
   d. Jean Jacques Rousseau

3. The *Encyclopedia*
   a. set forth the most advanced critical ideas in religion, government, and philosophy
   b. inspired the support of the church
   c. represented a plea for freedom of expression
   d. both a and c

4. In the eyes of the *philosophes*, the chief enemy of the improvement of humankind was
   a. absolute despotism
   b. the church
   c. enlightened despotism
   d. Deism

5. According to the *philosophes*, the doctrine of original sin suggested that
   a. improvement of human nature on earth was impossible
   b. predestination as a doctrine was illogical
   c. the church was out of touch with the concerns of common people
   d. all of the above

6. Deists believed that
   a. God did not exist
   b. nature did not provide evidence of a rational God
   c. the existence of God could be deduced from a contemplation of nature
   d. both a and b

7. According to the Deists,
   a. there was no life after death
   b. rewards and punishments would be meted out in the afterlife according to the virtue of the life a person led on earth
   c. the fanaticism of various Christian sects could be overcome by reason and tolerance
   d. both b and c

8. Who took the lead in championing the cause of religious toleration during the Enlightenment?
   a. Voltaire
   b. the Huguenots
   c. Adam Smith
   d. Baron de Montesquieu

9. *The Wealth of Nations* by Adam Smith challenged the
   a. concept of scarce goods and resources
   b. economic theory of mercantilism
   c. special trading monopolies and the regulation of labor
   d. all of the above

10. *Laissez-faire* economic thought and policy argued in favor of

a. government intervention and regulation of the economy
   b. a very limited role for government in the economic life and regulation of a state
   c. private management of all aspects of community life such as schools and maintenance of roads
   d. both b and c

11. In *The Spirit of the Laws*, Montesquieu argued that
    a. a single set of enlightened political laws could regulate all human societies
    b. a republic was the best form of government for human societies
    c. the good political life depended on the relationship of many political variables
    d. the aristocracy was a hindrance to the proper functioning of a government

12. One of Rousseau's most influential ideas
    a. involved a separation among the different branches of government
    b. defended the control of a properly organized society over its members
    c. was that morality in society was unimportant
    d. saw individualism as the most important component of society

13. The *philosophes* on the whole
    a. were strong feminists
    b. advocated radical changes in the social condition of women
    c. were not strong feminists
    d. both a and b

14. The most extensive political, religious, and social programs associated with enlightened absolutism were carried out by
    a. Maria Theresa of Austria
    b. Joseph II of Austria
    c. Catherine the Great of Russia
    d. both b and c

15. Catherine the Great
    a. carried out limited reforms on her own authority
    b. attempted to maintain ties of friendship and correspondence with the *philosophes*
    c. continued the economic program and diplomatic policies of Peter the Great
    d. all of the above

16. The Scientific Revolution
    a. never involved more than a few hundred people
    b. swiftly changed European culture
    c. had little impact on moral or religious issues
    d. replaced Christianity as the worldview of Europeans

17. Nicolaus Copernicus
    a. completely rejected Ptolemaic astronomy
    b. was motivated by new astronomical data
    c. was motivated to construct a more mathematically elegant basis for astronomy
    d. both a and c

18. Galileo articulated the concept of a universe
    a. that was ultimately mysterious and unpredictable
    b. totally subject to mathematical laws
    c. governed by mutual attraction
    d. knowable through empirical induction

19. Francis Bacon was one of the first European writers to
   a. champion innovation and change
   b. question the Ptolemaic worldview
   c. insist that scientific thought must be mathematically elegant
   d. criticize the new science

20. Descartes divided existing things into the categories of
   a. matter and form
   b. empirical and mathematical
   c. things thought and things occupying space
   d. things occupying space and things outside of time and space

21. In the natural sciences, Descartes' deductive methodology
   a. lost favor to induction
   b. became the standard scientific method
   c. led to great advances in knowledge and technology
   d. both b and c

22. For Isaac Newton, the final test of any theory was whether
   a. it made sense
   b. it described what was actually observed
   c. it was mathematically elegant
   d. both a and c

23. Most of the scientists during the Scientific Revolution
   a. rejected Christianity
   b. were devout Christians
   c. believed that science and religion had nothing to do with each other
   d. became agnostic

24. One of Montesquieu's most important ideas was
   a. the elimination of the aristocracy
   b. the elimination of the monarchy
   c. the division of powers
   d. both a and c

25. Joseph II of Austria
   a. extended freedom of worship to Lutherans, Calvinists, and Greek Orthodox
   b. allowed Jews to worship privately
   c. sought to control the Roman Catholic Church
   d. all of the above

When

1. Based on the number of significant publications, which decades were the most important in the Enlightenment?

2. Place in correct order: Charter of Nobility, First Partition of Poland, death of Catherine the Great, death of Peter the Great, Russia annexes Crimea, Treaty of Kuchuk-Kainardji.

Where

After viewing Map 23-2 on page 508 of the textbook, how specifically was Poland eradicated? Which country benefited the most from territory accumulated by the partition? Why was Poland unable to survive the onslaught of Prussia, Russia, and Austria?

How and Why

1. Choose three of the following and discuss each one's contribution to the Scientific Revolution: Copernicus, Galileo, Kepler, Bacon, Newton, and Brahe. Which of the three made the most important contribution and why?

2. How did the Enlightenment change basic Western attitudes toward reform, faith, and reason? What were the major formative influences on the *philosophes*? How important were Voltaire and the *Encyclopedia* in the success of the Enlightenment?

3. Why did the *philosophes* consider organized religion to be their greatest enemy? Discuss the basic tenets of Deism. What criticisms might Deists find in traditional Christianity and how might they improve it?

4. Discuss the economic ideas of mercantilism and compare and contrast those ideas with the ideas of Adam Smith. Which set of ideas is more influential today?

5. Were the enlightened monarchs true believers in the ideals of the *philosophes* or was their enlightenment a mere veneer? Were they really absolute in power? What motivated their reforms? What does the partition of Poland indicate about the spirit of "enlightened absolutism"?

Map Labeling

Study Map 23-1 on page 507 of your textbook. On the map provided for you on the next page draw the boundaries of Russia in 1689 and shade in the areas added between 1689 and 1796.

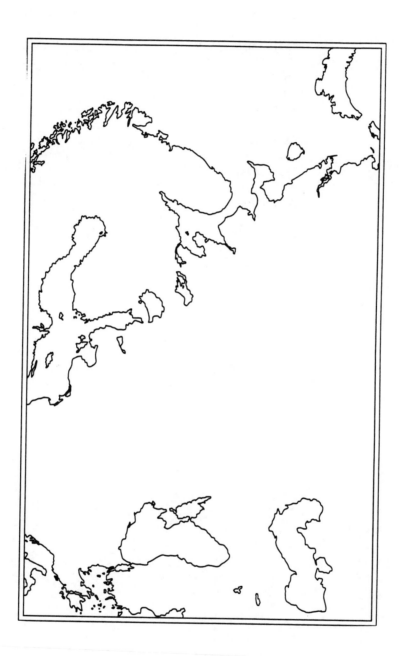

MULTIPLE CHOICE ANSWER KEY *(with page references)*

1. C (496)
2. C (499)
3. D (500)
4. B (501)
5. A (501)
6. C (501)
7. D (501)
8. A (501)
9. D (503)
10. B (503)
11. C (503)
12. B (504)
13. C (505)
14. D (505)
15. D (507)
16. A (496)
17. C (497)
18. B (497)
19. A (498)
20. C (498)
21. A (498)
22. B (498)
23. B (499)
24. C (503)
25. D (506)

Chapter Twenty-Four
Revolutions in the Transatlantic World

Practice Test

1. France's economic problem during the eighteenth century was that
    a. the government was unable to tap the wealth of the nation
    b. its accumulated debt was overly large given its economic vitality
    c. its accumulated debt was disproportionate to the debts of other European powers
    d. both a and b

2. The abolition of slavery in the transatlantic world
    a. occurred in 1750
    b. was a temporary phenomenon, since slavery existed in the British empire in 1890
    c. was one of the most permanent achievements unleashed by the Enlightenment
    d. was due to the solitary efforts of the Methodists

3. The National Assembly
    a. broke away from the Estates General
    b. voted by class, not by head
    c. prevented the First and Second Estates from voting on laws
    d. met within the Bastille for symbolic reasons

4. In the Tennis Court Oath, members of the National Assembly swore to
    a. meet until they had given France a constitution
    b. provide France with an economic plan for reducing the deficit
    c. grant every French citizen freedom of speech and assembly
    d. protect the nation by instituting a general draft for military purposes

5. Which of the following was a factor in the destruction of the Bastille in 1789?
    a. the mustering of royal troops in the city
    b. famine and the outbreak of bread riots
    c. the citizen militia of Paris was collecting arms
    d. all of the above

6. Peasant disturbances in the countryside during July and August of 1789 were called the
    a. *journees*   c. Great Fear
    b. Thermidorian Reaction   d. July Days

7. The *Declaration of the Rights of Man* proclaimed that
    a. the Estates General was defunct
    b. all citizens were to be equal before the law
    c. all citizens were to be presumed innocent until proof of guilt
    d. both b and c

8. On October 5, 1789, Parisian women marched to Versailles and demanded that
    a. the king's head be cut off   c. the king be deposed
    b. the king return to Paris   d. women be included in the National Assembly

9. The Civil Constitution of the Clergy
    a. assured the independence of the clergy from state control
    b. was the major blunder of the National Constituent Assembly
    c. was fully supported by the pope
    d. both a and c

10. The Creole elite in Latin America feared that
    a. a liberal monarchy in Spain would impose reforms that would hurt their economic interests
    b. a Spanish monarchy controlled by France would drain the region of wealth and resources
    c. local juntas would depose them from power
    d. both a and b

11. Haiti achieved independence in 1804 following a slave revolt led by
    a. San Martín
    b. Jose de Guayaquil
    c. Toussaint L'Ouverture
    d. Father Hidalgo

12. The Thermidorian Reaction
    a. resulted in the death of Robespierre
    b. tempered the violent extremes of the Terror
    c. was instituted by the Treaty of Basel
    d. caused food riots throughout Paris

13. Napoleon's concordat with Pope Pius VII in 1801
    a. resulted in religious dominance for the Catholic church in France
    b. forced the clergy to swear an oath of loyalty to the state
    c. allowed that clergy would be paid by the pope
    d. none of the above

14. The Napoleonic Code of 1804
    a. resulted in full political equality for French citizens
    b. allowed labor unions to represent urban workers
    c. provided for full legal equality between men and women
    d. none of the above

15. The chief aim of the Congress of Vienna was to
    a. prevent a recurrence of the Napoleonic nightmare
    b. arrange an acceptable settlement for Europe that would bring lasting peace
    c. codify the political gains of the French revolution and promote freedom throughout Europe
    d. both a and b

16. The *Commonwealthmen*
    a. believed that standing armies were instruments of tyranny
    b. believed that standing armies were essential to national security
    c. defended the Stamp Act
    d. supported George III

17. After the Treaty of Paris in 1763 the British were faced with
    a. the loss of colonies
    b. the cost of empire
    c. the need to organize a vast new territory
    d. both b and c

18. The British ministry of Lord North
    a. worked for a compromise with the American colonies
    b. asserted the authority of Parliament over the colonies
    c. included colonial representation in Parliament
    d. both b and c

19. During the War of the American Revolution, the colonies were aided by
    a. France and Germany
    b. Spain and Germany
    c. France and Spain
    d. France and Sweden

20. At first, the American colonists saw themselves as
    a. preserving traditional English liberties
    b. rejecting English political traditions
    c. developing a new sense of liberty
    d. both b and c

21. The sans-culottes were
    a. radical Jacobins
    b. counter-revolutionaries
    c. working class Parisians
    d. supporters of the national Constituent Assembly

22. The dechristianization policies of the Convention
    a. unified radical Paris with the countryside
    b. was welcomed in the provinces
    c. aroused opposition in the provinces
    d. was made permanent by Napoleon

23. In 1802, the Treaty of Amiens
    a. disbanded the Second Coalition
    b. made peace between Napoleon and the Roman Catholic Church
    c. recognized Egypt as a French colony
    d. brought temporary peace to Europe

24. Unable to defeat the British navy, Napoleon
    a. became allied with Great Britain
    b. waged economic war with Great Britain
    c. fomented rebellion in the Americas
    d. ignored Great Britain

25. Brazilian independence
    a. came about relatively peacefully
    b. was won in a long and bloody war with Portugal
    c. was won by Simon Bolivar
    d. both b and c

When

1. Between June 1789 and August 1795, how many governments were established in France?

2. For how long was the Cult of Reason the official religion of France?

3. Put the following in correct order: Boston Tea Party, Sugar Act, Treaty of Paris, First Continental Congress, Stamp Act, Declaration of Independence.

4. From the slave revolt in Haiti to the Battle of Ayacucho, how long did it take for Spain to lose its American empire?

Where

Using Map 24-1 on page 512 of your textbook, answer the following questions.

1. Name the original 13 colonies.

2. How large was the Indian Reserve relative to the 13 colonies?

How and Why

1. A motto of the French Revolution was "equality, liberty, and fraternity." How did the revolution both support and violate this motto?

2. How and why was Robespierre able to come to power and institute the Terror? What political and social changes were instituted as a result of the Thermidorian reaction?

3. Discuss Napoleon's rise to power. What challenges did the Directory face? How was Napoleon able to put out a constitution in 1799? What does Napoleon's early life and rise to power tell you about the man? Could a contemporary have predicted his greatness?

4. How important were San Martín, Bolívar, and other military leaders to Latin American independence movements in the 1820s?

5. How and why was the transatlantic slave trade abolished in the eighteenth and nineteenth centuries? Discuss specifically the process of abolition. What were the most important antislavery forces?

6. Who were the principal personalities and what were the most important problems of the Congress of Vienna? What were the results and why were they significant?

Map Labeling

In 1815, the Congress of Vienna restructured the territorial boundaries of post-Napoleonic Europe. Locate the following places on Map 24-2 provided on page 526 of your textbook and on the next page.

1. East Prussia
2. Austrian Empire
3. France
4. Kingdom of Sardinia
5. Russian Empire
6. Hanover
7. Bavaria
8. Ottoman Empire
9. Netherlands
10. Kingdom of the Two Sicilies

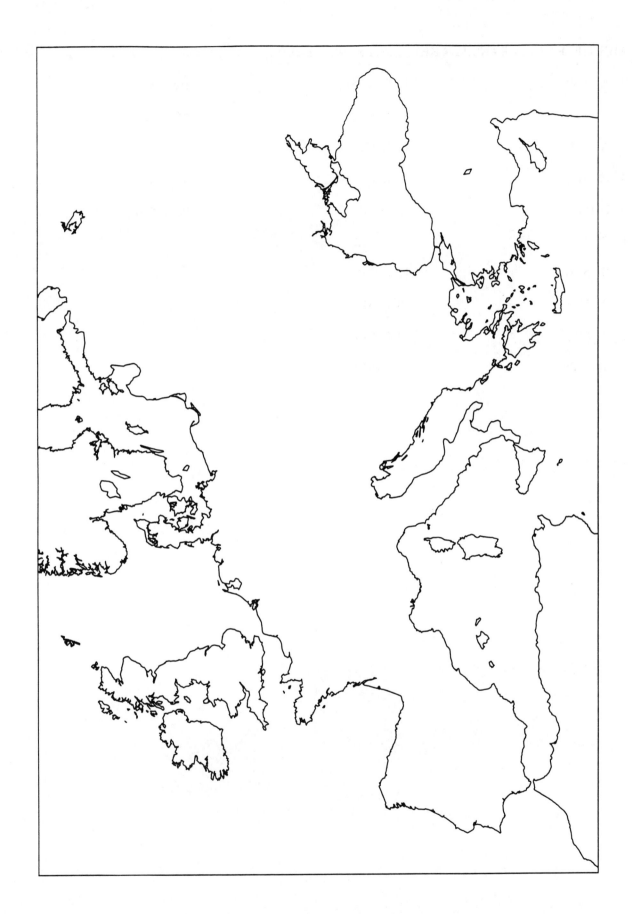

MULTIPLE CHOICE ANSWER KEY *(with page references)*

1. A (514)
2. C (530)
3. A (514)
4. A (514)
5. D (514)
6. C (514)
7. D (515)
8. B (515)
9. B (515)
10. D (528)
11. C (528)
12. B (521)
13. B (523)
14. D (523)
15. D (525)
16. A (512)
17. D (512)
18. B (513)
19. C (513)
20. A (513)
21. C (519)
22. C (521)
23. D (522)
24. B (523)
25. A (530)

Chapter Twenty-Five
Political Consolidation in Nineteenth-Century Europe and North America, 1815-1880

Practice Test

1. The Compromise of 1850
    a. upset the South and created instability
    b. demonstrated the weakening of pro-slavery advocates
    c. restored political calm and stability and reassured the South
    d. none of the above

2. Politically, the July Monarchy in France was
    a. more liberal than the Bourbon restoration government
    b. more conservative than the Bourbon restoration government
    c. very responsive to the demands of the lower and working classes
    d. both a and c

3. During the 1820s, the Catholic Association argued for
    a. union with Great Britain
    b. an eight-hour work day
    c. Catholic emancipation from Great Britain
    d. an end to Catholic representation in Parliament

4. The Catholic Emancipation Act of 1829
    a. resulted in the political independence of Ireland
    b. allowed Catholics to become members of Parliament
    c. seemed to create an Anglican monopoly on British political life
    d. allowed all Irish citizens to vote

5. The Four Ordinances of 1830
    a. enlarged the French electorate
    b. created the Chamber of Deputies
    c. eliminated the hereditary monarchy
    d. none of the above

6. The suppression of the Decembrist Revolt in 1825 benefited which of the following monarchs?
    a. Louis XVIII
    b. Nicholas I
    c. Charles X
    d. Louis Philippe

7. The Great Reform Bill of 1832 sought to
    a. provide a Charter, or constitution, for the French Catholics
    b. abolish "rotten" boroughs and create more urban electoral districts
    c. establish legal rights for Roman Catholics in Britain
    d. unite Scotland and Britain as one nation

8. The revolutions of 1848 were caused by
    a. food shortages and famine due to poor harvests
    b. widespread unemployment
    c. liberal demands for civil liberty, unregulated economic life, and representative government
    d. all of the above

9. The Kansas-Nebraska Bill of 1854
    a. rejected the principle of popular sovereignty
    b. renewed the national debate over slavery
    c. divided the antislavery forces
    d. prevented warfare against slaveholding settlers in Kansas

10. The Dred Scott decision of 1856
    a. repealed the Compromise of 1850
    b. effectively repealed the Missouri Compromise
    c. radicalized the South
    d. limited the idea of popular sovereignty

11. The Crimean War
    a. was fought among Austria, Russia, and Prussia
    b. resulted in a clear-cut victory for Russia
    c. was the first conflict to use poisonous gas
    d. shattered the image of an invincible Russia

12. Camillo Cavour
    a. sought to drive the Austrians out of Italy by force
    b. was a moderate liberal in economic matters
    c. wanted to establish a republican government in Italy
    d. both a and c

13. The single most important political development in Europe between 1848 and 1914 was the
    a. unification of Italy
    b. annexation of Schleswig and Holstein to Germany
    c. construction of a united German nation
    d. destruction of the Prussian Parliament

14. Otto von Bismarck pursued a *kleindeutsch* solution to the question of unification, which
    a. excluded Austria from German affairs
    b. included Austria in German affairs
    c. demanded the return of Alsace-Lorraine to Germany from France
    d. sought the augmentation of the German army through a tax increase

15. The *Ausgleich*, or Compromise of 1867,
    a. declared that the Austrian empire would halt its expansion
    b. transformed the Habsburg empire into a dual monarchy
    c. resulted in the deposition of Francis Joseph as Austrian emperor
    d. crowned Louis Kossuth as Hungarian king

16. Nationalism is based on
    a. the historical fact of distinct races in Europe
    b. adherence to a constitution
    c. the modern concept that political and ethnic boundaries should coincide
    d. both a and c

17. Nationalists
    a. opposed the political principles of the Congress of Vienna
    b. protested the existence of multinational states
    c. objected to ethnic groups dwelling in political units smaller than the ethnic nation
    d. all of the above

18. A significant difficulty of nationalism was, and is,
    a. determining which ethnic groups could be considered nations
    b. the lack of popular support for nationalism
    c. the stability of conservative, dynastic regimes
    d. the violence often associated with nationalistic groups

19. European liberals derived their political ideals from
    a. the Congress of Vienna
    b. the Enlightenment
    c. ancient Greek models
    d. the *Declaration of Independence*

20. European liberals
    a. were democrats
    b. worked to help the lower classes
    c. believed in privilege based on wealth and property
    d. supported political rights for women

21. The liberal concept of individual rights
    a. had no application outside of Europe and North America
    b. was used throughout the world in support of various causes
    c. was permanently discredited during the revolutions of 1848
    d. flourished only in the United States

22. The leader of the Irish movement for home rule was
    a. William Gladstone
    b. Benjamin Disraeli
    c. the Duke of Wellington
    d. Charles Stewart Parnell

23. The dynamic for change in 1848 originated with
    a. nationalists
    b. liberals
    c. the working class
    d. conservatives

24. The triumph of conservative forces in 1848
    a. ended the era of liberal revolution
    b. influenced the modernization of Japan
    c. led to a new era of urban riots led by the working class
    d. both a and b

25. Self-government in Canada
    a. led to a uniformly English culture
    b. was the result of rebellion against Great Britain
    c. was initiated by Great Britain
    d. both a and c

Where

Under the leadership of Otto von Bismarck, Prussia was able to unite the various German states into the nation of Germany. Study Map 25-3 on page 556 of your textbook. How specifically did Bismarck unite the grey section from 1866-1867 as the North German Confederation? By what diplomatic or military means did he unite the Bavarian section in 1871? Why did he desire Alsace and Lorraine after the Franco-Prussian War of 1871?

How and Why

1. What factors, old and new, led to the widespread outbreak of revolution in 1848? Were the causes in the various countries essentially the same or did each have its own particular set of circumstances? What was the response to the revolutions? Why did they fail?

2. What were the tenets of liberalism? Who were the liberals and how did liberalism affect the political developments of the early nineteenth century?

3. Why was the Crimean War fought? Who were the participants and how did the results of the war affect European history in subsequent years?

4. Why was it so difficult to unify Italy? What groups were urging unification? Who was Cavour and how did he achieve what others had failed to do? What was Garibaldi's contribution to Italian unification?

5. What was Bismarck's policy of unification and why did he succeed? What effect did the unification of Germany have on the rest of Europe?

Map Labeling

Examine Map 25-4 on page 559 of your textbook. The Habsburg Empire included a patchwork of nationalities and ethnic groups. Identify the following nationalities or ethnic groups on the map provided on the next page by shading in the appropriate areas:

1. Germans
2. Hungarians (Magyars)
3. Italians
4. Romanians
5. Czechs
6. Slovaks
7. Poles
8. Ukrainians
9. Serbs
10. Croats
11. Slovenes

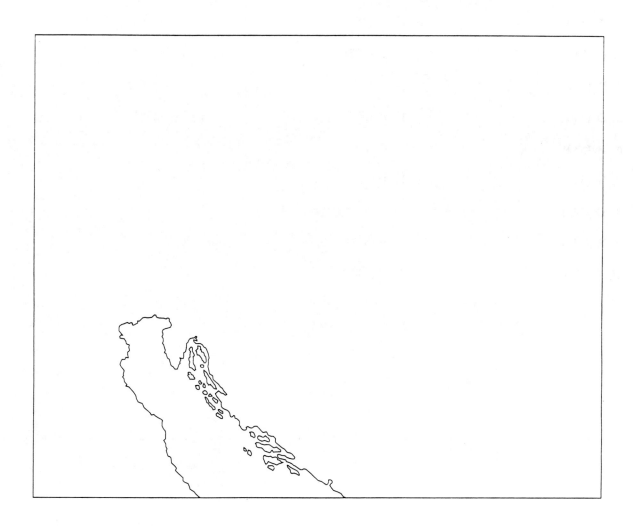

MULTIPLE CHOICE ANSWER KEY *(with page references)*

1. C (547)
2. A (540)
3. C (541)
4. B (541)
5. D (540)
6. B (539)
7. B (541)
8. D (543)
9. B (547)
10. B (547)

11. D (552)
12. B (553)
13. C (555)
14. A (551)
15. B (558)
16. C (536)
17. D (536)
18. A (537)
19. B (537)
20. C (537)

21. B (538)
22. D (542)
23. B (543)
24. D (544)
25. C (551)

Chapter Twenty-Six
Northern Transatlantic
Economy and Society, 1815-1914

Practice Test

1. Proletarianization refers to
    a. patronage of workers by the owner of a factory
    b. the gradual control of workers in setting the wages and working conditions for a factory
    c. the gradual loss of workers' ownership of the means of production and control over their own trades
    d. the gradual lowering of the cultural level of society due to the influx of the poor into urban areas

2. The New Immigrants around the turn of the century
    a. came primarily from southern and eastern Europe
    b. assimilated quickly and had remarkable upward social mobility
    c. supplied labor for the agricultural boom of the period
    d. both a and c

3. Women were paid low wages because
    a. they rarely had to support themselves independently
    b. they usually lived in their parents' home
    c. there were more jobs than women to fill them
    d. none of the above

4. One of the most important social changes to occur during the nineteenth century was the
    a. restriction of Jews throughout European society
    b. emancipation of European Jews from the ghetto to nearly equal social status
    c. legal restriction of Jews in Eastern Europe as opposed to freedom in the West
    d. none of the above

5. Zionism refers to
    a. attacks on Jewish life by European governments
    b. the movement to establish a Jewish state in Palestine
    c. a majority movement within the Jewish community for full legal rights throughout Europe
    d. a terrorist movement led by the Russian Jewish community

6. From the middle of the nineteenth century, the middle and working classes
    a. sought housing within the center of the city because of its convenience
    b. moved to rural areas and often took up farming as an occupation
    c. sought housing in suburbs which were less expensive and less congested
    d. both b and c

7. Confection refers to the
    a. production of goods in standard sizes
    b. production of custom made goods by artisans as a means of competing with factories
    c. proliferation of small business in factory towns
    d. attempt to increase production and lower wages to become competitive with factories

8. Which of the following major developments in the second half of the nineteenth century affected the economic lives of women?
    a. married women sought to enter the work force in significant numbers
    b. opportunities as teachers became limited as governments sought to restrict public education
    c. women were paid a comparable wage to men
    d. there was an expansion in the variety of available jobs for women

9. Which of the following contributed to the exploitation of women workers outside the home?
    a. the definition of the chief work of women to be in the mills
    b. the expectation of separate social and economic spheres for men and women
    c. the rise in prostitution
    d. the legal restriction of women to a small number of occupations

10. The Progressives
    a. were generally supportive of the efforts of Big Business
    b. wanted to see more efficient and less corrupt government
    c. had little impact on state and local government
    d. worked carefully with rural reform populist leaders

11. Who of the following was a radical feminist and suffragette?
    a. Emmeline Pankhurst   c. Marie Mauguet
    b. Hubertine Auclert   d. all of the above

12. The advent of democracy in most major European states witnessed the formation of
    a. trade unions   c. organized mass political parties
    b. literacy laws   d. laws to restrict the franchise to a political elite

13. The American Federation of Labor
    a. sought to transform the life of workers in a radical fashion
    b. was organized among nonskilled labor
    c. was led by Samuel Gompers
    d. all of the above

14. The Erfurt Program of 1891
    a. rejected socialist principles and advocated sustained capitalism
    b. declared the doom of capitalism and the necessity of socialist ownership of production
    c. was fully supported by Otto von Bismarck
    d. both a and c

15. V. I. Lenin's political faction was called the
    a. Mensheviks   c. Zemstvos
    b. Bolsheviks   d. Soviets

16. In the second half of the nineteenth century
    a. Europe developed states with large electorates and political parties
    b. the president became the center of American political life
    c. women became politically active in Europe and the U.S.
    d. all of the above

17. By 1830
    a. all of northwestern Europe had become a fully industrial society
    b. only the U.S. had become a fully industrial society
    c. only Great Britain had become a fully industrial society
    d. no state had yet become a fully industrial society

18. Urban artisans in the nineteenth century
    a. experienced proletarianization more slowly than factory workers
    b. experienced proletetarianization more quickly than factory workers
    c. did not experience proletarianization
    d. disappeared as factories made them obsolete

19. The cholera epidemics of the 1830s and 1840s
    a. struck only the poor
    b. were thought to have been spread by miasmas in the air
    c. initiated a broad concern for public health
    d. both b and c

20. Reformers believed that the terrible living conditions of the poor
    a. were caused by immorality and laziness
    b. would cause political trouble
    c. could be improved without government involvement
    d. both a and c

21. The industrial economy
    a. reinforced traditional gender roles
    b. was most beneficial to women
    c. transformed gender roles
    d. both b and c

22. Middle-class women
    a. were more limited in their roles than women of other classes
    b. were less limited in their roles than women of other classes
    c. were not subject to arranged marriages
    d. could vote

23. Liberal society and law
    a. presented women with many obstacles
    b. provided feminists with many of their political and intellectual tools
    c. encouraged equality
    d. both a and b

24. Europe's most advanced women's movement was in
    a. France
    b. Great Britain
    c. Germany
    d. Russia

25. According to the *Communist Manifesto*
    a. class conflict is the engine of historical development
    b. revolution is not historically necessary
    c. capitalism is the culmination of human history
    d. there will always be class conflict

When

1. When and where were women first allowed to vote on national issues? When were women allowed to vote in Germany? In Great Britain?

2. Put the following in correct order: founding of the British Labour Party, founding of the German Social Democratic Party, founding of the Fabian Society, founding of the First International, founding of the French *Confederation Generale du Travail*.

3. How long did each of the first three Russian *Dumas* sit before they were dismissed?

How and Why

1. How and why did the middle class change in its political and social outlook before 1848 to its posture about 1875?

2. What was the status of women in the second half of the nineteenth century? Why did they grow discontented with their lot? To what extent had they improved their position by 1914? What tactics did they use? Was the political emancipation of women inevitable?

3. Discuss the relationship of the labor movement and the socialist movement in any two of the following countries: Britain, France, and Germany. In which country was the cooperation between the two closest? Least? Why?

4. What was the status of the industrial proletariat in 1860? Had it improved by 1914? What caused the growth in trade unions and organized mass political parties? How did Europe's socialist movement respond to these administrations?

5. How would you define Progressivism? What were the goals and demands of the Progressives? Who were its leading exponents and how did Progressivism change from 1900 to 1920?

MULTIPLE CHOICE ANSWER KEY *(with page references)*

1. C (568)	11. D (582)	21. C (573)
2. A (592)	12. C (585)	22. A (580)
3. D (574)	13. C (593)	23. B (581)
4. B (583)	14. B (587)	24. B (581)
5. B (584)	15. B (590)	25. A (586)
6. C (570)	16. D (568)	
7. A (569)	17. C (568)	
8. D (577)	18. A (569)	
9. B (579)	19. D (571)	
10. B (594)	20. B (573)	

Chapter Twenty-Seven
Latin America:
From Independence to the 1940s

Practice Test

1. During the nineteenth and early twentieth centuries, Latin America was similar to Africa and Asia. In all three regions,
    a. particular nations or areas would specialize in a niche in the world economy
    b. vast mining industries extracted mineral resources
    c. foreign niche economies were exploited throughout the world
    d. both a and b

2. No matter what conflict existed among the literate political and economic elites of Latin America, they
    a. stood united in their opposition to any substantial social reform
    b. all believed in granting civil liberties to all persons
    c. all decided to abolish slavery throughout Latin America by 1855
    d. extended the right to vote without property qualification

3. After the Wars of Independence in the early nineteenth century, Creole elites
    a. redistributed land among the peasants
    b. experienced domestic opposition and social revolution
    c. refused to make changes in landholding arrangements
    d. both a and b

4. After the Wars of Independence
    a. Latin America experienced a period of general prosperity
    b. only Brazil prospered
    c. all Latin American countries abolished slavery
    d. liberal democracies became the norm

5. The political philosophies embraced by the educated and propertied Creole elite
    a. made them more sensitive to the social and economic needs of the peasantry
    b. allowed them to legislate political freedoms that had been supported by the *philosophes*
    c. favored the protection of property and ignored the social problems of the poor
    d. both a and b

6. The late-nineteenth-century European theories of "scientific" racism
    a. did not take root in Latin America
    b. were used to preserve the Latin American status quo
    c. attributed the economic backwardness of Latin America to climatic problems
    d. none of the above

7. How did the conservative intellectual heritage inherited from Europe play an important role in twentieth-century Latin American political thought?
    a. in the insistence of military groups to view themselves as the guarantors of order
    b. in the desire to formulate constitutions based on Enlightenment values
    c. in the opposition of the political elites to the intrusion of Communism
    d. both a and c

8. By the 1920s,
    a. the U.S. had become the dominant trading partner of Latin America
    b. Great Britain had become the dominant trading partner of Latin America
    c. Latin America had gained control of its economic destiny
    d. Latin America was less dependent on the export of raw materials and food products

9. Latin American economies during the early twentieth century can best be described as
    a. supply-side economies
    b. Keynesian economies
    c. neocolonial economies
    d. import-deprived economies

10. A *caudillo* in Latin America usually
    a. came from the peasant class of society
    b. supported liberal causes such as land redistribution
    c. came from the officer corps or enjoyed military support
    d. was controlled by the Catholic church

11. Argentina became a republic with a federal constitution when
    a. Juan Manuel de Rosas was overthrown 1852
    b. Juan Perón assumed power in 1943
    c. Hipolito Irigoyen was elected in 1916
    d. Julio Roca concluded a peace agreement after his *Conquest of the Desert* in 1879

12. Throughout the 1930s, a right-wing nationalistic movement arose among writers called
    a. *Semana Tragica*
    b. *nacionalismo*
    c. *Cinco de Mayo*
    d. *La Reforma*

13. Porfirio Díaz maintained one of the most successful dictatorships in Latin America by
    a. focusing his attention on the needs of the peasantry
    b. redistributing the lands of the *haciendas*
    c. giving almost every political sector something it wanted
    d. allying closely with the Catholic church

14. The Plan of Ayala called for
    a. the removal of U.S. companies from Mexico
    b. the redistribution of land to peasants
    c. an end to "Dollar Diplomacy"
    d. the institution of a Communist government in Mexico

15. The Vargas years from 1930 to 1945 represent a major turning point in Brazilian history because he
    a. was a pragmatist who survived by changing his policies and political alliances in order to remain in power
    b. disbanded the Brazilian military
    c. supported a constitution democracy without equivocation
    d. both b and c

16. The limited prosperity of Latin America was based on
    a. slave labor
    b. economic isolation
    c. the export of agricultural commodities and raw materials
    d. the export of finished goods

17. The European concept of *positivism*
    a. helped spread democracy in Latin America
    b. was popular among scientists and politicians
    c. was popular among the military elite
    d. challenged the traditional social order

18. The term *mestizo* refers to
    a. person of Native American and European descent
    b. a person of African and European descent
    c. a person of African and Native American descent
    d. any mixed race person in Latin America

19. Import substitution included
    a. industries that transformed raw materials for export
    b. industries addressing local demand
    c. industries that transformed imported materials
    d. all of the above

20. Which of the following technological advances helped make Argentina one of the wealthiest nations in Latin America?
    a. the automating of the sugar harvest
    b. refrigerated ships
    c. railroads
    d. both b and c

21. Which of the following can be regarded as the supreme twentieth-century embodiment of the *caudillo*?
    a. Emilio Zapata
    b. Juan Peron
    c. Juan Manuel del Rosas
    d. Porfirio Diaz

22. *La Reforma* refers to
    a. the movement against Santa Anna's autocracy in Mexico
    b. the socially progressive policies of Juan Peron in Argentina
    c. the abolition of slavery in Brazil
    d. the land reform policies of Zapata and Villa

23. In which of the following ways did Brazil differ from other nations in the region?
    a. its heritage and language were Portuguese
    b. it retained slavery
    c. it had a highly unstable government
    d. both a and b

24. The Brazilian Republic was able to run smoothly from 1891 to 1930 because
    a. it allowed many people to vote
    b. it diversified the economy
    c. it eliminated the influence of the wealthy landowners
    d. of the arrangement among the regional governors

25. The children of immigrants to Argentina
    a. zealously maintained the culture of their home countries
    b. often became the strongest nationalists in the twentieth century
    c. became wealthy landowners
    d. formed the basis for the Radical Party

When

1. How long after the development of ship refrigeration was the conquest of the desert complete? What is the relationship between these two events?

2. For how long was coffee the dominant crop in Brazil?

3. Place the following in correct order: Organization of the PRI, beginning of Mexican civil war, invasion of Mexico by the French, defeat of Mexico by the U.S., era of Porfirio Diaz.

Where

Using Map 27-1 on page 601 of your textbook, match the city with the Latin American state.

1. Veracruz_____   A. Empire of Brazil

2. Montevideo_____   B. Chile

3. Santiago_____   C. Mexico

4. Caracas_____   D. Uraguay

5. Rio de Jainero_____   E. Gran Colombia

How and Why

1. How did Latin America develop political independence from colonial powers without revolution? What was the role of the Creole elite in this process? Why was there not a fundamental revolution in the area until 1910? What was the role of the Roman Catholic church in the process of revolution in Latin America?

2. How did the landowners of Latin America retain their respective control after the independence movement? What was the importance of "scientific" racism in this process? How were the British important in developing certain economies that supported the landowning elite?

3. What was the role of the *caudillo* in developing Latin American governments after independence? Why did the army and the landowners support these figures? Why did democratic governments fail to develop in the region?

4. Describe the political development from independence to 1945 of two of the following three countries: Brazil, Argentina, and Mexico. How were they similar and how did they differ? Why was Mexico unique in its political development?

5. Why did industrialization not develop in Latin America as it did in Europe and in the United States? What role did the price of land play in this process? Why was foreign capital not used to build an industrial base in any of the countries?

6. Why was the emancipation of the slaves delayed until 1888 in Brazil? What role did the slave trade have on the overall economic structure of the country? After the emancipation, did the economic structure change a great deal?

Map Labeling

By 1830, new sovereign states had emerged following the Wars of Independence that freed Latin America from Iberian rule. Identify these states on Map 27-1 on page 601 of your textbook and place them on the map provided on the next page.

1. Chile
2. Mexico
3. British Honduras
4. Empire of Brazil
5. Uruguay
6. Bolivia
7. Gran Columbia
8. United Provinces of La Plata
9. Paraguay
10. United Provinces of Central America
11. Peru
12. Haiti

MULTIPLE CHOICE ANSWER KEY *(with page references)*

1. D (600)	11. A (606)	21. B (608)
2. A (600)	12. B (607)	22. A (609)
3. C (600)	13. C (609)	23. D (611)
4. B (600)	14. B (610)	24. D (612)
5. C (600)	15. A (613)	25. B (607)
6. B (603)	16. C (604)	
7. D (603)	17. C (603)	
8. A (604)	18. A (603)	
9. C (605)	19. D (605)	
10. C (605)	20. D (606)	

Chapter Twenty-Eight
India, the Islamic Heartlands, and Africa:
The Encounter with the Modern West (1800-1945)

Practice Test

1. The expression "the impact of modernity" refers to the
    a. desecration of Eastern philosophical ideals by Western writers
    b. effect on traditional cultures of the introduction of social, economic, technological, scientific, and ideological forms of "modern" Western civilization
    c. impact of imperialism on traditional cultures in Africa and Asia
    d. none of the above

2. As early as a half-century before the British crown asserted direct rule over India in 1858, the British wielded effective imperial control
    a. by blockading Indian ports with merchant ships
    b. through Indian "clients" who were paid by British companies
    c. through the East India Company
    d. by controlling overland trade with Asia

3. In the face of mismanagement and misuse of their land by British merchants, Indians
    a. were passive and did not revolt against such abuse
    b. were active in resistance by promoting almost constant revolt
    c. blamed Muslim farm workers and launched the Sepoy massacre
    d. never resorted to peasant movements of noncooperation

4. The Revolt of 1857 was triggered by
    a. concern among Bengali troops about animal grease on their rifles
    b. the beating death of a Bengali soldier
    c. excessive tax rates for Bengali troops
    d. a failure to pay mercenary Bengali troops on time

5. The "Mutiny" of 1857
    a. was a nationalist revolution
    b. presaged the rise of an effective unified Indian opposition to the British
    c. demonstrated an underlying resentment by Indians to the burdens of foreign domination
    d. both b and c

6. The policy of the British East India Company
    a. did not officially include cultural imperialism
    b. adamantly in favor of cultural imperialism
    c. so oppressive that the British crown decided to rule India directly
    d. both b and c

7. In the nineteenth century, the most influential member of the Indian elite to engage the British was
    a. Mohandas K. Gandhi   c. Ram Mohan Roy
    b. B. G. Tilak   d. G. K. Gokhale

8. The most important *jihad* movement at the beginning of the nineteenth century was led by
    a. Mahatma Gandhi   c. Usman Dan Folio
    b. The Mahdi   d. Muhammad Bello

9. The impact of British ideas in India
    a. was limited to a small but influential elite
    b. influenced a wide segment of the population
    c. especially revitalized the Hindu population
    d. both a and c

10. The advent of the British crown *raj* in India in 1858 occurred because of
    a. a change of government control in Britain from Whig to Tory
    b. the *Sepoy* Rebellion of 1857-1858
    c. the oppression of the British East India Company
    d. the Opium Wars

11. The "founder of Pakistan" who led Muslims to separatism from India was
    a. Jawaharlal Nehru   c. Sayyid Ahmad Khan
    b. Muhammad Ali Jinnah   d. Muhammad Iqbal

12. The Tanzimat reforms were
    a. intended to bring the Ottoman state into line with ideals espoused by European states
    b. intended to give European powers less cause for intervention in Ottoman affairs
    c. designed to regenerate confidence in the Ottoman state from its own people
    d. all of the above

13. The most extreme example of an effort to modernize and nationalize an Islamic state following a Western model can be found in the
    a. creation of the Turkish republic out of the ashes of the Ottoman state after World War I
    b. creation of the Pakistani state in 1947
    c. rise to power of the Saudi royal house in Arabia
    d. none of the above

14. In southern Africa, the *mfecane* era in the first quarter of the nineteenth century was characterized by
    a. the rise of trade among tribes
    b. internal cooperation and unity of tribes in opposition to white incursions
    c. a population increase due to medical efforts on the part of Europeans
    d. devastating internal warfare, depopulation, and forced migrations

15. The Great Trek of *voortrekers* between 1835 and 1841
    a. brought 6,000 Afrikaners south into Cape Colony from Natal
    b. resulted in the death of almost all the Afrikaners who participated
    c. resulted in the creation after 1850 of the Orange Free State
    d. all of the above

16. In West Africa, the slave trade was replaced by
    a. demand for palm oil and gum arabic
    b. demand for coffee and palm oil
    c. European investment in infrastructure
    d. both a and c

17. In Africa, the nineteenth century is notable for
    a. the fixing of Christianity as a permanent part of the African scene
    b. the decline of Islam
    c. the fixing of Islam as a permanent part of the African scene
    d. a return to indigenous religion

18. Christian missionaries in Africa
    a. were often instruments of imperialism
    b. sought to provide Africans with medicine and education
    c. provided Africans with the principles to use against their exploiters
    d. all of the above

19. In Africa, the British
    a. preferred direct colonial administration
    b. preferred indirect colonial administration
    c. were less enlightened rulers than the French
    d. both a and c

20. By World War I all of Africa was under European control except
    a. Somalia
    b. Liberia
    c. Ethiopia
    d. both b and c

21. The national consciousness of the various African colonies was based on
    a. long-standing tribal identities
    b. opposition to European rule
    c. a shared commitment to Islam
    d. an intellectual elite trained in African universities

22. Cantonments
    a. segregated white masters from natives in India
    b. were camps set up by European missionaries in Africa
    c. were areas of native self-rule in colonial territories
    d. fostered diversity in the British Raj

23. The first prime minister of India was
    a. Mohandas Gandhi
    b. Ram Mohan Roy
    c. B.G. Tilak
    d. Jawaharal Nehru

24. The Wahhabis
    a. brought about a Shi'ite revival in Iran
    b. emphasized inner piety and puritanical external practice
    c. helped revive Ottoman rule
    d. encouraged compromise between Islam and Western ideas

25. Jamal al-Din al-Afghani is best known
    a. as the father of modern Afghanistan
    b. for encouraging a return to traditional Islamic political structures
    c. for his emphasis on pan-Islamism
    d. as the father of modern Pakistan

When

1. How long did the Indian National Congress exist before India was granted independence?

2. Put the following in correct order: the Great Trek of the Boers, the *mfecane,* the creation of the Orange Free State and the South African Republic, the reign of Shaka, the British annexation of the Natal, the Britsh conquest of the Cape Colony.

Where

Use Map 28-1 on page 631 of your textbook to answer the following questions.

1. Which European state controlled the most African territory?

2. Which European state controlled the least African territory?

3. Great Britain wished to build a railroad from Egypt to Cape South Africa. Which other European state would have to cooperate with such a project?

How and Why

1. What does "the impact of modernity" mean to traditional cultures of the Afro-Asian-Indian world? What was the general reaction of the native populations? Why was the West so successful in imposing its will on these areas of the world?

2. Why was India called the "jewel" in the crown of the British empire? How did the British gain control of the India subcontinent? How did the British develop the area economically? Why was there little attempt to bring the native population in as equal rulers with the British?

3. In what manner was the Islamic world divided after 1800? How did these divisions influence the arrival of European powers? Why was there a failure of unity against European states after 1855?

4. How did Islamic nationalism affect European control in Africa, Asia, and the Near East? How and where did nationalism develop? Why was there only one successful "national" state after 1918 in these regions of the world?

5. Discuss the new African states and power centers of sub-Saharan Africa before 1870. Why was there a failure to develop a modern state in the area? What was the role of Islam in the development of these political units? What role did trade play in developing an economic base in the region?

Map Labeling

By 1914, nearly the whole of Africa was partitioned by European powers. Only Liberia and Abyssinia remained independent. Identify the following locations on Map 28-1 on page 631 of your textbook and place them on the map provided on the next page. Also, name the colonizing country for each of the locations.

1. Egypt/Sudan
2. Somaliland
3. Angola
4. Southwest Africa
5. Algeria
6. Libya
7. Gold Coast
8. Abyssinia
9. Eritrea
10. East Africa
11. Congo
12. Mozambique
13. South Africa
14. Rhodesia
15. Sierra Leone
16. Liberia
17. Morocco
18. Nigeria

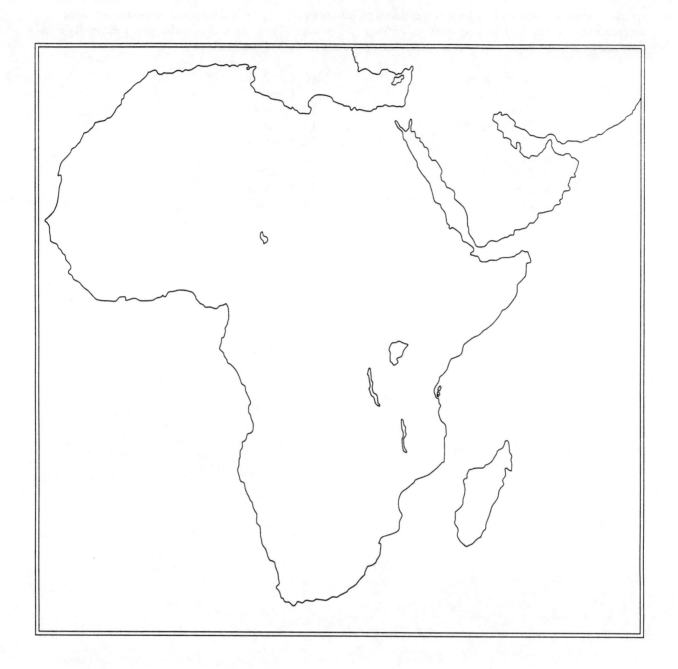

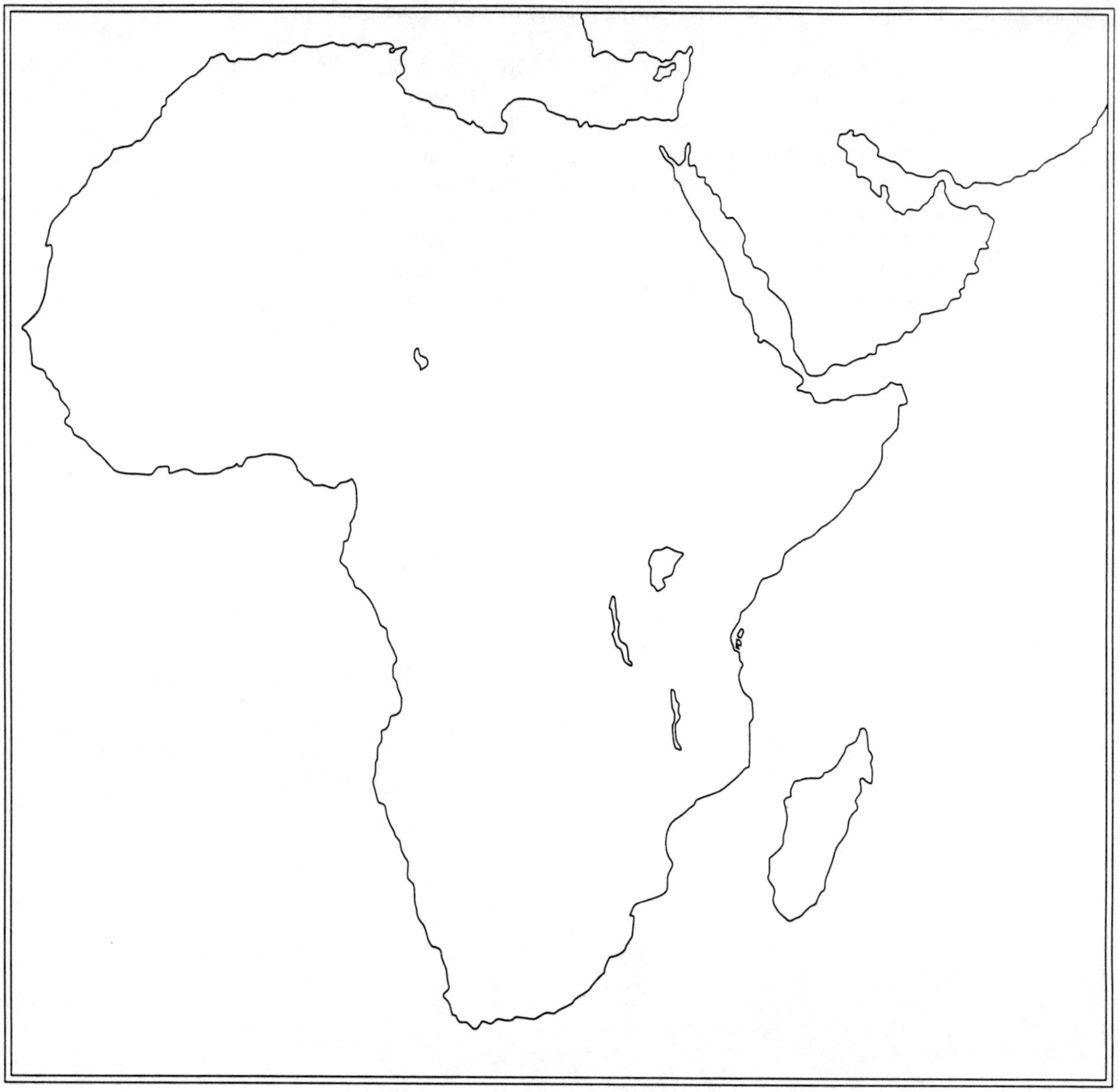

MULTIPLE CHOICE ANSWER KEY *(with page references)*

1. B (618)
2. C (618)
3. B (619)
4. A (619)
5. D (619)
6. A (619)
7. C (619)
8. C (628)
9. A (619)
10. B (619)

11. B (622)
12. D (625)
13. A (625)
14. D (627)
15. C (627)
16. A (628)
17. C (628)
18. D (630)
19. B (630)
20. D (630)

21. B (633)
22. A (620)
23. D (621)
24. B (623)
25. C (626)

Chapter Twenty-Nine
Modern East Asia

Practice Test

1. A rapid political change took place in Japan in 1853-1854 with the coming of
    a. Confucian leadership
    b. Commodore Matthew Perry
    c. the Meiji administration
    d. the Tokugawa regime

2. By 1910, Japan
    a. had been defeated by China
    b. had defeated China and Russia
    c. had been defeated by Russia
    d. both a and c

3. After the Opium War, China
    a. immediately began to modernize
    b. immediately overthrew the ruling dynasty
    c. was held by tradition and refused political reform for 70 years
    d. both a and b

4. The Treaty of Nanking in August of 1842
    a. was the first of the "unequal treaties"
    b. ended the "tribute system"
    c. provided Britain with Hong Kong, a huge indemnity, and five new ports
    d. all of the above

5. Between 1850 and 1873, China
    a. endured a series of rebellions that reduced population significantly
    b. opened up its economy to the West with the arrival of Matthew Perry
    c. fought the Opium War with Great Britain
    d. underwent a major political change in the ruling dynasty

6. The Taiping ideology
    a. was influenced purely by ancient Chinese texts
    b. included the sharing of property and prohibition of opium, alcohol, and adultery
    c. allowed prostitution, tobacco consumption, and gambling
    d. none of the above

7. The single most influential reformist thinker in China was
    a. the empress dowager Tz'u-hsi
    b. K'ang Yu-wei
    c. Tseng Kuo-fan
    d. Hung Hsiu-ch'uan

8. The treaty ports of China by the 1860s were
    a. little islands of privilege and luxury for foreigners
    b. bastions of cruelty where native Chinese were physically abused
    c. never very safe, as property was often confiscated and extortion was the rule
    d. both b and c

9. The term Hermit Kingdom was applied because of its isolation to
    a. Vietnam
    b. Manchuria
    c. Japan
    d. Korea

10. Sinkiang
    a. means "New Territories"
    b. means "Eastern Capital"
    c. was cause of war between China and Japan
    d. was the center of Communist support in China

11. The primary leader of the Kuomintang was
    a. Mao Tse-tung
    b. Tseng Kuo-fan
    c. Chiang Kai-shek
    d. Ch'en Tu-hsiu

12. The Meiji period in Japan was an attempt to
    a. revert back to Japanese political and social traditions of the eighteenth century
    b. create a modern state and to progress on a level with the West
    c. eliminate political parties as cumbersome and inefficient
    d. institute a "modern Shogunate" with centralized authority and minimal political freedom

13. The basic weakness of the Japanese political democracy in the early to mid-1920s was
    a. a failure to promote universal education and literacy
    b. an economic depression that caused unemployment and suffering
    c. lack of growth in the railroads and other transportation industries
    d. the cultural and social gap between the military and the civilian elite

14. The general who led Japan to World War II was
    a. Tojo Hideki
    b. Katsura Taro
    c. Kato Komei
    d. Hara Takashi

15. The Japanese decided to attack Pearl Harbor in 1941 because
    a. their alliance with Hitler demanded it
    b. they could not take the Dutch East Indies with the United States in the Philippines
    c. they believed that American productivity of war material was not as great as their production
    d. none of the above

16. The founder of the KMT was
    a. Chiang Kai-Shek
    b. Mao Tse-tung
    c. Sun Yat-sen
    d. Yuan Shih-k'ai

17. During the Long March
    a. Chiang Kai-shek defeated the Communists
    b. the Japanese conquered China
    c. Mao Tse-tung founded the Communist Party
    d. Mao Tse-tung assumed leadership of the Communist Party

18. The war between Japan and China which began in 1937
    a. was part of a Chinese plan to reassert control over Korea
    b. began with an unplanned skirmish at Peking
    c. was part of a Japanese plan to conquer China
    d. was an opportunity for the KMT

19. In the first few years after Perry opened Japan
    a. the Tokugawa political system collapsed
    b. the *bakufu* signed a commercial treaty with the U.S.
    c. little changed
    d. the imperial court signed a commercial contract with the U.S.

20. The immediate goal of the Meiji leaders was to
    a. centralize political power
    b. abolish the samurai class
    c. establish political parties
    d. both a and b

21. Under the Japanese constitution the lower house of the Diet had the authority to
    a. approve budgets
    b. appoint the prime minister
    c. pass laws
    d. both a and c

22. A major goal of the Meiji state was to
    a. strengthen the military
    b. implement democracy
    c. raise the standard of living
    d. protect individual rights

23. The rise of militarism in the 1930s in Japan
    a. was inevitable
    b. was the original goal of the Meiji reforms
    c. might not have happened without the Great Depression
    d. both a and b

24. The Japanese army took over Manchuria
    a. as the first phase of an overall imperial policy
    b. to maintain a buffer between the Soviet Union and Korea
    c. at the invitation of the local warlord
    d. as part of the treaty ending the Russo-Japanese War

25. The goals of the Tripartite pact were to
    a. isolate the U.S.
    b. inherit the southeast Asian colonies of the European powers
    c. improve relations with the Soviet Union
    d. all of the above

When

1. Put the following in the correct chronological order: Taiping Rebellion, May Fourth Movement, "self-strengthening" movement

2. How long after the arrival of Perry did it take Japan to adopt a Western-style constitution? To defeat China in a war? To defeat Russia in a war?

Where

Use Map 29-1 on page 654 of your textbook to answer the following questions.

1. Which three states were involved in the competition for dominance in Northeast Asia?

2. Why do you think Port Arthur and the Kwangtung Peninsula were strategically important?

How and Why

1. Describe the similarities and differences in Chinese and Japanese responses to Western influence. Why was Japan more open to foreign concepts than was China? What was the role of nationalism in this issue?

2. Why did the rebellions from 1850 to 1873 fail in China? What were the major objectives of the Taiping movement? How many people were involved and why was there such extensive damage to the population and to the countryside? What steps were taken by the government to recover from this period in Chinese history?

3. Describe the formation of the Kuomintang Party and its influence on Chinese history. Who were its leaders? Why did the Chinese Communist Party leave the organization? In what areas of China did the KMT have its strength? What was the impact of the war with Japan on the party?

4. What were some of the major goals of the Meiji state in Japan? How did some of their programs differ from other reforms in Japanese history? What were the golden years of Meiji?

5. How and why did Japan become involved in World War II? Why did they suffer defeat in this war? Explain the nature of Japanese fascism and compare it with German Nazism.

Map Labeling

Study Map 29-1 on page 654 of your textbook. Using the blank map on the next page, identify the extent of the Japanese empire in 1910. Shade in territories acquired by the Japanese between 1910-1933. Finally, identify and label the following cities: Port Arthur, Peking, Seoul, Nanking, Tokyo, and Hong Kong.

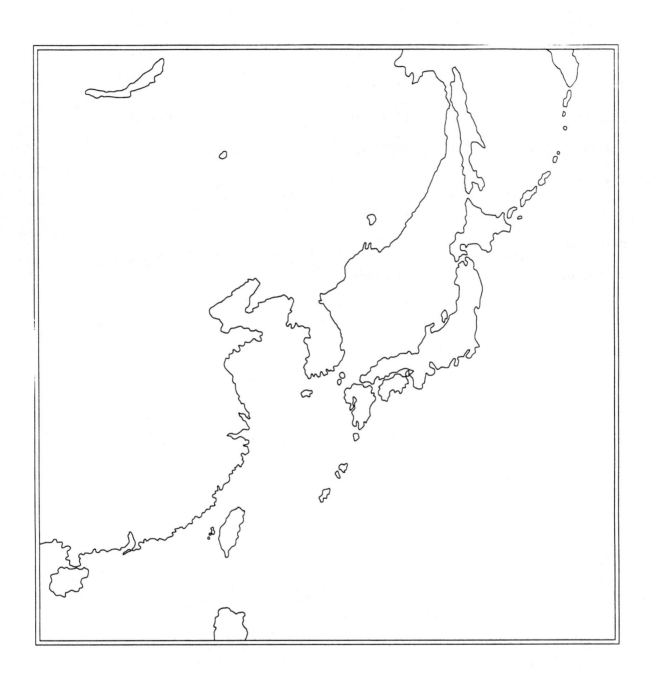

MULTIPLE CHOICE ANSWER KEY *(with page references)*

1. B (638)
2. B (638)
3. C (639)
4. D (638)
5. A (639)
6. B (639)
7. B (642)
8. A (640)
9. D (640)
10. A (640)
11. C (645)
12. B (649)
13. D (656)
14. A (658)
15. B (660)
16. C (644)
17. D (645)
18. B (646)
19. C (647)
20. A (649)
21. D (650)
22. A (651)
23. C (653)
24. B (657)
25. D (659)

**Chapter Thirty
Imperialism and World War I**

Practice Test

1. Which of the following best describes the motives of the "New Imperialism"?
    a. the search for new markets and raw materials
    b. strategic and political considerations
    c. the desire to export surplus populations
    d. there is still no agreement about the motives for the "New Imperialism"

2. The Three Emperors' League of 1873
    a. consisted of Germany, Austria, and Russia
    b. collapsed in 1877 because of the Austrian occupation of Bosnia
    c. collapsed in 1877 as a result of uprisings in the Ottoman Balkan provinces
    d. both a and c

3. European diplomacy was revolutionized in 1871 by the
    a. death of the Austrian Arch-Duke Francis Ferdinand
    b. death of German Chancellor Otto von Bismarck
    c. creation of the German empire
    d. both a and c

4. According to the Treaty of San Stefano in 1878,
    a. Russia lost control of the Balkans
    b. Slavic states in the Balkans were freed from Ottoman rule
    c. the European balance of power was stabilized
    d. the Dardanelles fell under British control

5. Until 1890, Bismarck guided German policy and insisted that
    a. Germany was a satisfied power and wanted no further territorial gains
    b. Britain reduce the size of its navy
    c. France cede to Germany the areas of Alsace and Lorraine
    d. France remove its colonies from East Africa

6. The Dual Alliance of 1879 provided
    a. that if either Germany or Austria were attacked by Russia, the other ally would intervene
    b. for economic free trade between Germany and Austria
    c. that Russia would be excluded from all European affairs
    d. for a blank check of support from Germany for Austrian desires in the Balkans

7. Why did Britain not join the Triple Alliance?
    a. Britain was already committed to the Entente Cordiale
    b. Britain clung to its policy of "splendid isolation"
    c. the First Moroccan Crisis prevented British involvement in formal alliances
    d. the Franco-Russian alliance was troublesome to the British and they opposed its intent

8. The Entente Cordiale of 1904
    a. was a formal military treaty between Britain and France
    b. settled all outstanding colonial differences between France and Britain
    c. was another name for the Triple Entente
    d. none of the above

9. The main result of the Second Moroccan Crisis was that
    a. Britain ceded part of the Congo to Germany
    b. Germany set up a permanent base in Agadir
    c. Britain lost control of the Suez Canal
    d. British fear of Germany increased, and this drew Britain closer to France

10. On June 28, 1914, a young Bosnian nationalist touched off World War I by assassinating
    a. Kaiser William
    b. Archduke Francis Ferdinand
    c. Chancellor Bethmann-Hollweg
    d. General von Moltke

11. Germany's grand strategy for quickly winning the war against France
    a. involved a *Blitzkrieg* attack into Alsace
    b. demanded the invasion of Russia before attacking France
    c. was called the Schlieffen Plan
    d. focused on the destruction of the Maginot Line in France

12. In 1915, the sinking of the British liner *Lusitania* by a German submarine
    a. brought America into the war against Germany
    b. encouraged the German policy of unrestricted submarine warfare throughout the war
    c. allowed Woodrow Wilson to ship war materials to Britain
    d. none of the above

13. The Russian Provisional Government in 1917 was led by
    a. V. I. Lenin
    b. Leon Trotsky
    c. Alexander Kerensky
    d. Joseph Stalin

14. The Treaty of Brest-Litovsk in 1917
    a. confirmed the Bolsheviks in power
    b. yielded Poland, the Ukraine, and the Baltic states to France
    c. produced peace between "Red" and "White" Russian political factions
    d. took Russia out of World War I

15. The League of Nations was unlikely to be effective because
    a. there were no armed forces at its disposal
    b. any action required unanimous consent of its council
    c. Germany and the Soviet Union were excluded from the League Assembly
    d. all of the above

16. The usual pattern of the New Imperialism was for the European nation to
    a. transform the economy and culture of a country through investment
    b. transform the economy and culture of a country by helping the country industrialize
    c. conquer a country through force of arms
    d. foment rebellion in a country to topple its government

17. The motive for the New Imperialism was
    a. economic
    b. strategic
    c. prestige
    d. all of the above

18. Austria and Germany learned from the Balkan wars that
    a. better results might be obtained by international conferences
    b. the use of force was counterproductive
    c. better results might be obtained through the use of force
    d. both a and b

19. The outbreak of war in Europe in 1914 was greeted with
    a. fear
    b. jubilation
    c. indifference
    d. relief

20. Italia Irredenta refers to
    a. the motto of the Italian Republic
    b. Italians living outside a united Italy
    c. The Austro-Hungarian policy towards its Italian minority
    d. Sicily

21. One of the deterrents to an earlier American intervention in WWI was
    a. ethnic and culture similarities between Americans and Germans
    b. the presence of Great Britain among the Allies
    c. the presence of France among the Allies
    d. the presence of Russia among the Allies

22. Wilson's idealism during the settlement at Paris
    a. conflicted with the war aims of the other victors
    b. provided a unifying vision for the victors
    c. was shared by Great Britain
    d. allowed for the inclusion of the war guilt clause

23. The greatest immediate threat to peace in 1919 appeared to be
    a. nationalism
    b. Bolshevism
    c. fear of Germany
    d. fear of France

24. The war guilt clause
    a. justified forcing Germany to pay huge reparations to the victors
    b. caused bitter resentment among the Germans
    c. was one of Wilson's 14 points
    d. both a and b

25. In the west, the main territorial issue was the fate of
    a. Turkey
    b. France
    c. Austria-Hungary
    d. Germany

When

Put the following events in order: Bosnian Crisis, Russo-Turkish War, Congress of Berlin, creation of the German empire, Dual Alliance, Russo-Japanese War, Franco-Russian Alliance, Entente Cordiale, Bismarck dismissed.

Where

1. According to Map 30-1 on page 670 of your textbook, which imperialist powers lost influence and/or territory in Asia between 1880-1914? Which ones gained influence and/or territory?

2. Study Map 30-4 on page 684 of your textbook and compare it with Map 30-2 on page 676. How did the borders in Western and Eastern Europe change from 1914 to 1919 with the settlement of the Treaty of Versailles? Pay particular attention to the division of the German empire and the creation of new states in the Balkan region. Why did Russia lose areas on its western border?

How and Why

1. To what areas of the world did Europe extend its power after 1870? How and why did European attitudes towards imperialism change after 1870? What features differentiate the "New Imperialism" from previous imperialistic movements? What features do they have in common?

2. What was the Schlieffen Plan and what was it intended to accomplish? Why did it fail? Had it succeeded, would the Germans have won World War I?

3. What role in the world did Bismarck envisage for the new Germany after 1871? How successful was he in carrying out his vision? Why? What was Bismarck's attitude toward colonies? Was he wise to tie Germany to Austria-Hungary?

4. How did developments in the Balkans lead to the outbreak of the war? What was the role of Serbia? Austria? Russia? What was the aim of German policy in July 1914? Did Germany want a general war?

5. Why was Lenin successful in establishing the rule of the Bolsheviks? What role did Trotsky play? Was Lenin right in taking Russia out of the war?

6. Assess the settlement of Versailles. What were its good points? bad points? Was the peace too harsh or too conciliatory? Could it have ensured peace in Europe? How might it have been improved?

Map Labeling

The main theaters of activity in World War I were in the European arena. Identify the following locations on Map 30-2 on page 676 of your textbook and place them on the map provided on the next page.

1. German Empire
2. Austria-Hungary
3. Russia
4. Western Front
5. Italian Front
6. Russian Front
7. Serbia
8. France
9. Belgium
10. Italy
11. Ottoman Empire

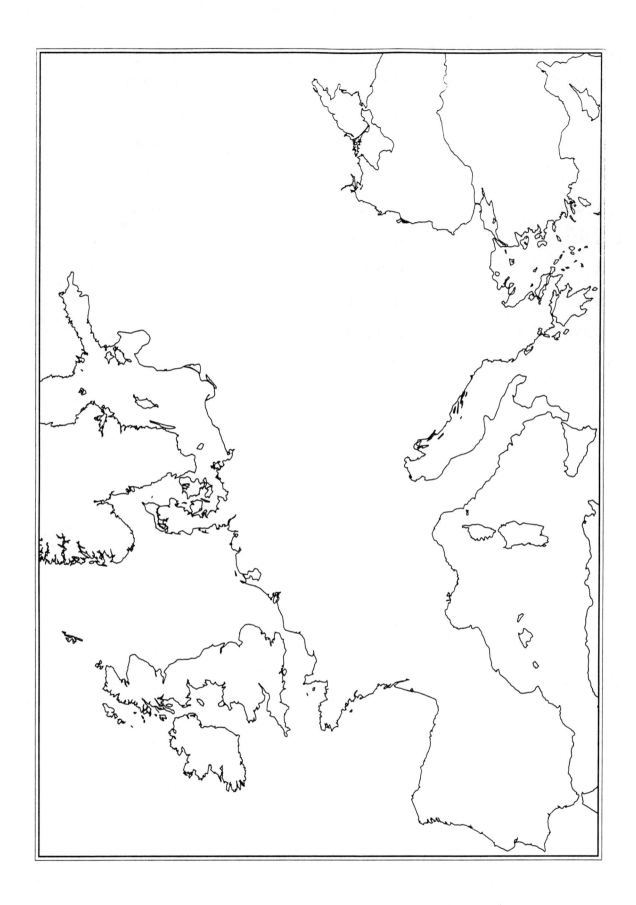

MULTIPLE CHOICE ANSWER KEY *(with page references)*

1. D (668)
2. D (669)
3. C (669)
4. B (669)
5. A (669)
6. A (671)
7. B (671)
8. B (672)
9. D (673)
10. B (674)

11. C (675)
12. D (678)
13. C (679)
14. D (679)
15. D (683)
16. A (668)
17. D (668)
18. C (674)
19. B (677)
20. B (677)

21. D (678)
22. A (681)
23. B (682)
24. D (685)
25. D (683)

Chapter Thirty-One
Depression, European Dictators, and the American New Deal

Practice Test

1. Which of the following accounted for the experimentation in politics and economic life in the two decades that followed the conclusion of World War I?
    a. new governments faced postwar political reconstruction
    b. the military provided stability for new regimes, which allowed them to experiment
    c. the Great Depression caused governments to experiment with solutions to postwar problems
    d. both a and c

2. The peace settlement at Versailles in 1919
    a. fostered a sense of stability and finality
    b. fostered both resentment and discontent in many European countries
    c. allowed Germany to recover gradually
    d. established stable political regimes throughout most of Europe

3. In 1923, France declared Germany in default of reparations payments and
    a. invaded the Ruhr mining district
    b. presented their case at the League of Nations, which forced Germany to pay its debts
    c. demanded the Dawes Plan, which brought international pressure on Germany
    d. proposed the Young Plan to institute harsher conditions on Germany

4. The Dawes Plan of 1924
    a. eased the German repayment of reparations
    b. brought international pressure on Germany to pay its debts to France
    c. contributed to the stock market crash of 1929
    d. none of the above

5. The most important French political experiment in the 1930s was the
    a. Vichy regime
    b. Popular Front Ministry
    c. Paris Commune
    d. Fabian Society

6. Which of the following are characteristics of a fascist government?
    a. democratic and constitutional
    b. antidemocratic, anti-Marxist, and frequently anti-Semitic
    c. antidemocratic, pro-Marxist, with a middle-class orientation
    d. democratic, but with a franchise limited to property owners

7. The leader of the *Fasci di Combattimento* was
    a. Gabriele D'Annunzio
    b. Camillo Cavour
    c. Benito Mussolini
    d. Giuseppe Garibaldi

8. In 1923, Hitler
    a. was elected to the *Reichstag* as a Social Democrat
    b. became an advisor to Gustav Stresemann
    c. met with Mussolini to develop strategy for the future
    d. was arrested because of an aborted beer hall *putsch*

9. The individual most responsible for the construction of the Weimar Republic was
    a. Paul von Hindenburg
    b. Erich Ludendorff
    c. Gustav Stresemann
    d. Friedrich Ebert

10. As a result of the Locarno Agreements of 1925
    a. France and Germany both accepted the western frontier established at Versailles
    b. Britain and Italy agreed to intervene against the aggressor if France or Germany violated the frontier or if Germany moved into the Rhineland
    c. France supported Germany's membership in the League of Nations
    d. all of the above

11. In 1933, passage of the following act by the *Reichstag* allowed Hitler to rule by decree:
    a. Emergency Decree
    b. Enabling Act
    c. *Schutzstaffel* Act
    d. Nuremburg Act

12. The *Cheka* was the
    a. Nazi secret police
    b. Soviet commune
    c. rival party to the *Bolsheviks*
    d. none of the above

13. The NEP provided for the
    a. considerable private economic enterprise in Lenin's new Soviet state
    b. regulation of wages and prices as a part of the New Deal
    c. electrification throughout the American south
    d. funding of state and local relief agencies in the United States

14. Stalin decided to eliminate
    a. five-year plans because they were not working
    b. *kulaks* because they were resisting collectivization
    c. *Pravda* because its propaganda was directed against him
    d. all of the above

15. The Soviet purges ostensibly began with the
    a. exile of Boris Pasternak
    b. massacre of *kulaks*
    c. convictions of the murderers of Sergei Kirov
    d. none of the above

16. The people who most consistently experienced terror during the Nazi regime were
    a. Gypsies
    b. women
    c. Slavs
    d. Jews

17. The Nazi's views concerning women
    a. were not in conflict with German society
    b. were supported only by men
    c. were supported by conservative women
    d. none of the above

18. The Nazis saw women as
    a. educators of the young
    b. preservers of cultural values
    c. preservers of racial purity
    d. all of the above

19. After World War I, the United States
    a. assumed the role of a world power
    b. was minimally involved in international affairs
    c. supported the League of Nations
    d. aggressively enforced the Treaty of Versailles

20. The most pervasive problem of the Great Depression was
    a. unemployment
    b. government intervention
    c. labor strikes
    d. bank fraud

21. The Great Depression was triggered by
    a. lack of capital investment
    b. unequal distribution of wealth
    c. financial collapse
    d. economic difficulties in Europe and Latin America

22. Through the New Deal
    a. the federal government continued its ever growing activity
    b. the federal government was far more active than it had ever been
    c. the unemployment problem was solved
    d. both b and c

23. The major crisis of the Weimer period was brought on by
    a. inflation
    b. government incompetence
    c. the 1920 putsch
    d. Article 48

24. Hitler's supporters came mainly from
    a. big business
    b. the lower middle class
    c. labor unions
    d. all of the above

25. Despite the violence and repression, the Soviet experiment appealed to
    a. intellectuals
    b. people living in European colonies
    c. those who opposed fascism
    d. all of the above

When

Between 1919-1936, which three years were the most pivotal? Rank your three choices in order of importance and explain your choices.

How and Why

1. Define the doctrine of fascism. How and why did the fascists succeed in obtaining power in Italy? What tactics did they use? To whom did they appeal? To what extent does Mussolini deserve the credit for success? To what extent did success depend on the effectiveness of the opposition?

2. Could the Weimar Republic have taken root in Germany or was its failure inevitable? Between 1919 and 1929, what were the republic's greatest weaknesses? strengths? To what extent did its fate depend on personalities rather than underlying trends?

3. Why did Lenin institute the New Economic Policy? Was it successful? Could the Russian Revolution have succeeded without Lenin? How important was he in changing the history of the twentieth century?

4. How did the depression affect Germany? Compare and contrast Hitler's economic policies with those applied in the United States. In what ways were Roosevelt and Hitler similar in their approach to the economic crisis of the 1930s? Discuss Hitler's rise to power between 1929 and 1934. Why was he successful? Was his dictatorship inevitable? In what ways were the political goals of Hitler and Roosevelt different?

5. Why did Stalin decide that the Soviet Union had to industrialize rapidly? Why did this require the collectivization of agriculture? What obstacles stood in the way of collectivization and how did Stalin overcome them?

MULTIPLE CHOICE ANSWER KEY *(with page references)*

1. D (690)
2. B (690)
3. A (690)
4. A (690)
5. B (691)
6. B (697)
7. C (700)
8. D (700)
9. C (700)
10. D (701)
11. B (703)
12. D (692)
13. A (692)
14. B (694)
15. C (696)
16. D (704)
17. C (704)
18. D (705)
19. B (705)
20. A (706)
21. C (706)
22. B (707)
23. A (699)
24. B (700)
25. D (696)

Chapter Thirty-Two
World War II

Practice Test

1. The initial problem that confronted Hitler when he took power was
    a. lack of popular support
    b. the resentment of the officer corps
    c. the fact that his power was not sanctioned by the Weimar constitution
    d. rebuild the military

2. Which of the following was a goal of Hitler during his political career?
    a. to unite the entire German people into a single nation
    b. to gain living space for the German *Volk* by taking it from the Slavs
    c. to purify the new Germany by removing the Jews
    d. all of the above

3. Why did Mussolini attack Ethiopia?
    a. to defy the League of Nations
    b. to avenge a humiliating defeat suffered by the Italians in 1896
    c. to gain new markets for Italy
    d. to gain control of the Suez Canal

4. What was the response of the French to Hitler's remilitarization of the Rhineland?
    a. they invaded the Ruhr mining district of Germany
    b. they were unified internally but feared an attack by Britain if they invaded Germany
    c. they lodged a protest with the League of Nations
    d. they decided to build the Maginot Line

5. In 1936, the Spanish republic was invaded by Falangist forces led by
    a. Francisco Franco   c. King Juan Carlos
    b. General Escobar   d. Francisco de Guzman

6. The *Anschluss* took place in 1938 and involved the
    a. annexation of the Sudetenland
    b. annexation of Danzig
    c. union of Germany and Austria
    d. incorporation of Alsace and Lorraine into the Reich

7. Neville Chamberlain was famous as prime minister of Britain for his policy of
    a. "Bread and Peace" within Europe
    b. the appeasement of German demands
    c. an Anglo-Soviet alliance on the eve of World War II
    d. guaranteeing the integrity of the Maginot Line in France

8. Stalin made a secret nonaggression pact with Germany because
    a. the Western powers meant for the Soviet Union to bear the burden of the war against Germany
    b. he resented being left out of the Munich agreement
    c. Hitler offered Soviet control of Czechoslovakia
    d. both a and b

9. As a result of the Nazi-Soviet pact in 1939, the Soviet Union received
    a. Czechoslovakia and Hungary
    b. part of Poland and the Baltic states
    c. Bessarabia and the Balkan regions
    d. none of the above

10. The Maginot Line was
    a. a defensive line extending from Switzerland to the Belgian frontier
    b. designed to protect Germany from any more French invasions after the Ruhr incident
    c. a defensive line designed to protect the Rhineland
    d. a group of forts which acted as a buffer between the Soviet Union and Germany

11. Blitzkrieg can best be described as
    a. "lightning warfare"
    b. air warfare
    c. a phony war
    d. defensive war

12. After the fall of France in 1940, Hitler left southern France in control of the Vichy regime led by
    a. Henri Pétain
    b. Jean Jaures
    c. Charles de Gaulle
    d. Marc Bloch

13. The "Final Solution" refers to Hitler's policy of
    a. exiling Jews
    b. restricting Jews legally
    c. identifying Jews by marking them
    d. none of the above

14. On "D-Day" in 1944,
    a. there was an assassination attempt on Hitler
    b. Pearl Harbor was bombed by the Japanese
    c. Allied troops landed on the coast of Normandy
    d. France was liberated by the allies

15. At the Potsdam Conference in July 1945, the allied leaders present included
    a. Stalin, Churchill, and Roosevelt
    b. Atlee, Truman, and Stalin
    c. Churchill, Truman, and Stalin
    d. Stalin, Atlee, and Roosevelt

16. Hitler mobilized for total war
    a. prior to his invasion of Poland
    b. during the Anschluss
    c. after the Battle of Stalingrad
    d. because of the doctrine of Blitzkrieg, Germany never was forced to mobilize for total war

17. The major bombing campaigns over Germany
    a. undermined German morale
    b. did not undermine German morale
    c. were insignificant compared to the German bombing of Great Britain
    d. contributed to the Allied victory

18. Throughout the war years, opposition to Hitler in Germany
    a. was minimal
    b. was widespread
    c. led to a loss of industrial capacity
    d. never spread to the military

19. Most people in occupied and Vichy France were
    a. collaborators
    b. resistance fighters
    c. demoralized by defeat
    d. both a and c

20. For most people in Great Britain during the war
    a. the standard of living decreased
    b. bombing raids were a constant threat
    c. the standard of living rose
    d. both a and b

21. The first meeting between the leaders of the Allies took place in
    a. Tehran
    b. Potsdam
    c. Yalta
    d. Moscow

22. Operation Barbarosssa refers to
    a. the German plan to invade Great Britain
    b. the German plan to invade Russia
    c. the U.S. plan to invade Japan
    d. the U.S. strategy of island hoping

23. The Battle of Midway
    a. reversed the momentum of the war in the Pacific
    b. allowed the U.S. to devote more resources to the West
    c. allowed the U.S. to devote more resources to the East
    d. both a and b

24. No nation suffered more death and destruction during World War II than
    a. Japan
    b. Germany
    c. the Soviet Union
    d. France

25. As part of mobilizing for total war, the Nazis
    a. changed their views on women
    b. made extensive use of propaganda
    c. abandoned their racial policies
    d. both a and c

Where

On the eve of the German invasion of the Soviet Union in 1941, Germany and its ally Italy had formed a mighty empire by annexation, occupation, or alliance. Study Map 32-1 on page 713 of your textbook and Map 32-3 on page 717 of your textbook. When and how was Austria added to the German Reich? When was the Sudentenland incorporated? Why was Vichy France not occupied by the Germans? Compare this map with Map 32-4 on page 724 of your text. What changes had taken place in the empire between 1941 and 1945?

How and Why

1. What were Hitler's foreign policy aims? Was he bent on conquest in the east and dominance in the west, or did he simply want to return Germany to its 1914 boundaries?

2. Why did Britain and France adopt a policy of appeasement in the 1930s? What were its main features? Did the appeasers buy the West valuable time to prepare for war by their actions at Munich in 1938?

3. How was Hitler able to defeat France so easily in 1940? Why was the air war against Britain a failure? Why did Hitler invade the Soviet Union? Why did the invasion fail? Could it have succeeded?

4. Why did Japan attack the United States at Pearl Harbor? What was the significance of American intervention in the war? Why did the United States drop the atomic bombs on Japan? Did it make the right decision to do so?

Map Labeling

Study Map 32-3 on page 720 of your textbook. On the map provided for you shade in the area of the Japanese empire in 1931 and draw the border of the Japanese empire in 1942.

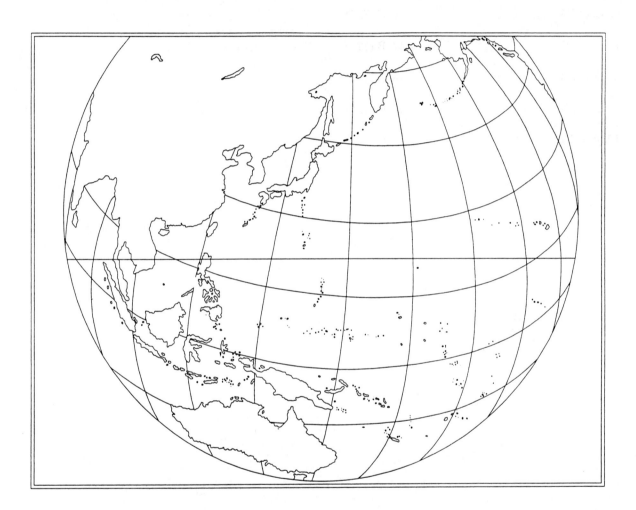

MULTIPLE CHOICE ANSWER KEY *(with page references)*

1. D (712)
2. D (712)
3. B (712)
4. C (713)
5. A (714)
6. C (714)
7. B (714)
8. D (715)
9. B (715)
10. A (716)

11. C (718)
12. A (716)
13. D (718)
14. C (719)
15. B (728)
16. C (722)
17. B (723)
18. A (724)
19. C (725)
20. C (726)

21. A (727)
22. B (718)
23. D (719)
24. C (726)
25. D (723)

Chapter Thirty-Three
The West Since World War II

Practice test

1. For 45 years after World War II, Europe
   a. maintained political unity
   b. remained artificially divided into eastern and western regions
   c. rejuvenated former colonial holdings
   d. participated in a gradual decay of democratic institutions

2. In the aftermath of World War II, Americans made no attempt to roll back Soviet power where it existed because
   a. American industrial power began to falter due to the war
   b. the United States wanted to establish its presence more fully in the East
   c. the United States found this consistent with their support of autonomy and democracy
   d. both b and c

3. In 1946, Winston Churchill gave a speech in Missouri that
   a. warned against Communist subversion
   b. spoke of an Iron Curtain descending over Europe
   c. urged Western unity and strength as a support to Stalin's subversion
   d. all of the above

4. According to the Truman Doctrine, the United States
   a. promised to aid free peoples resisting subjugation by outside pressures
   b. offered broad economic aid to European states on the condition that they work together
   c. offered to place the manufacture and control of atomic weapons under international control
   d. promised to roll back Soviet power in eastern Europe

5. In 1947, the United States gave aid to which of the following nations in its struggle against Communism?
   a. Poland   c. Greece
   b. Korea   d. Israel

6. The Marshall Plan in 1947
   a. provided broad economic aid to European states
   b. sought to free Eastern European countries from Soviet control
   c. promoted the policy of "containment"
   d. was designed to provide a constitution for Japan

7. The Suez Canal crisis of 1956 demonstrated that
   a. Americans could no longer impose their will on the rest of the world
   b. there was to be no more free trade between Egypt and the United States
   c. French and British forces could act efficiently in concert to control their empires
   d. none of the above

8. The Cuban missile crisis in 1962
   a. forced the United States to remove military bases from Cuba
   b. resulted in the U.S. blockade of Cuba and removal of Soviet missiles
   c. resulted in the installation of Soviet missiles in Cuba
   d. both a and c

9. The Helsinki Accords of 1975
    a. refused to recognize the Soviet sphere of influence in eastern Europe
    b. committed its signatory powers to recognize and protect the human rights of their citizens
    c. sanctioned the Soviet invasion of Afghanistan
    d. none of the above

10. The Velvet Revolution took place in
    a. Hungary under Imre Nagy
    b. Poland under Wladyslaw Gomulka
    c. Czechoslovakia under Vaclav Havel
    d. Czechoslovakia under Alexander Dubcek

11. In *Brown v. Board of Education of Topeka* (1954), the Supreme Court declared that
    a. segregation of the black and white races was unconstitutional
    b. separate but equal status between blacks and whites was constitutional
    c. prayer could not exist in public schools
    d. creationism could not be taught in schools

12. Under a policy called *perestroika*,
    a. Brezhnev quelled the Hungarian uprising
    b. Richard Nixon was allowed to visit the Soviet Union
    c. Gorbachev proposed major economic and political reforms
    d. none of the above

13. The policy of *glasnost*
    a. provided for a restructuring of government in the Soviet Union
    b. advocated the private ownership of land
    c. sanctioned the abandonment of traditional Marxist ideology
    d. allowed a broad public discussion and criticism of Soviet Communist policy

14. The Commonwealth of Independent States is
    a. an informal organization of the former British colonies
    b. a loosely organized federation of the 15 former Soviet republics
    c. a democratic organization that seeks international membership
    d. no longer existent

15. The Solidarity movement organized workers in
    a. Ukraine
    b. Poland
    c. Czechoslovakia
    d. Hungary

16. The events of 1956
    a. proved that European powers could still act independently
    b. ended the era of fully autonomous action by European nation-states
    c. revealed the internal weaknesses of the Soviet Union
    d. revealed the inability of the U.S. to translate military power into international influence

17. The Nuclear Test Ban Treaty
    a. marked the beginning of détente
    b. marked the end of détente
    c. concluded the Cuban Missile Crisis
    d. both a and c

18. The Treaty of Rome created
    a. a new European currency
    b. the European Coal and Steel Community
    c. NATO
    d. the European Economic Community

19. Eastern Europeans saw Western consumerism
    a. as the basic flaw in capitalism
    b. as clearly linked to democratic governments
    c. as possible in Communist states
    d. as unnecessary

20. The major motivation for migration within Europe from the late 1950s onward was
    a. political freedom
    b. fleeing from war
    c. economic opportunity
    d. to create more homogenous ethnic groupings

21. Under Communism women
    a. were considered property
    b. were not allowed to work outside the home
    c. enjoyed social equality
    d. participated in women's movements

22. The most important factor in creating new work patterns for women in postwar Europe was
    a. the lack of social equality
    b. longer life expectancies
    c. democratic governments
    d. the shortage of male workers

23. Lyndon Johnson's domestic program was called the
    a. New Deal
    b. Fair Deal
    c. War on Communism
    d. War on Poverty

24. Ronald Reagan
    a. established diplomatic relations with China
    b. was the first fully ideological conservative elected in the postwar era
    c. was the first fully ideological liberal elected in the postwar era
    d. both a and b

25. In the presidential election of 2000
    a. George W. Bush won the majority of the popular vote
    b. Al Gore won the majority of the electoral college vote
    c. Al Gore won the majority of the popular vote
    d. was decided by the House of Representatives

When

1. Put the following events into the correct order: Formation of Warsaw Pact, Soviet invasion of Afghanistan, Berlin Wall erected, Berlin Blockade, Solidarity founded, U-2 incident, formation of NATO, Helsinki Accords, Castro takes power in Cuba, Test Ban Treaty, Cuban missile crisis.

2. In which decade was the Cold War in most danger of becoming "hot"? Which events occurred in that decade that led you to your answer?

Where

Study Map 33-1 on page 735 of your textbook. Note carefully how European countries were divided into NATO and Warsaw Pact allies. Trace the "Iron Curtain" that Winston Churchill referred to in his famous speech. Why wasn't Yugoslavia included in the Warsaw Pact? Were these alliances voluntary organizations? How do these alliances reflect the bi-polar world of the Cold War?

How and Why

1. How did Europe come to be dominated by the two superpowers after 1945? Trace the stages of the Cold War. Why were 1956 and 1962 particularly crucial years? How strong an alliance is NATO today? How have the membership and purpose of the alliance changed?

2. What was the "Brezhnev Doctrine" and why did Gorbachev decide not to support it when he came to power? How did this decision affect Eastern Europe?

3. What social changes have taken place in Europe during the last half of the twentieth century? Focus on the migration of peoples, new patterns in the workforce, and the expectations of women.

4. How did the United States "reinvent" itself after the difficulties of Vietnam and Watergate? What role does the United States play in the world today?

5. Discuss the fall of the Soviet Union. What were the primary reasons that it could no longer remain a united polity? Why did Gorbachev fail to maintain his hold on power? Do you foresee decades of political instability? Why or why not?

Map labeling

The Soviet Union broke up into its 15 constituent republics in December 1991. Identify these republics on Map 33-2 on page 748 of your textbook and place them on the map provided on the next page.

1. Ukraine
2. Georgia
3. Turkmenistan
4. Kazakhstan
5. Russia
6. Latvia
7. Belorussia
8. Azerbaijan
9. Uzbekistan
10. Tadzhikistan
11. Armenia
12. Moldavia
13. Estonia
14. Lithuania
15. Kirghizia
16. Black Sea
17. Caspian Sea
18. Mediterranean Sea
19. Baltic Sea
20. China

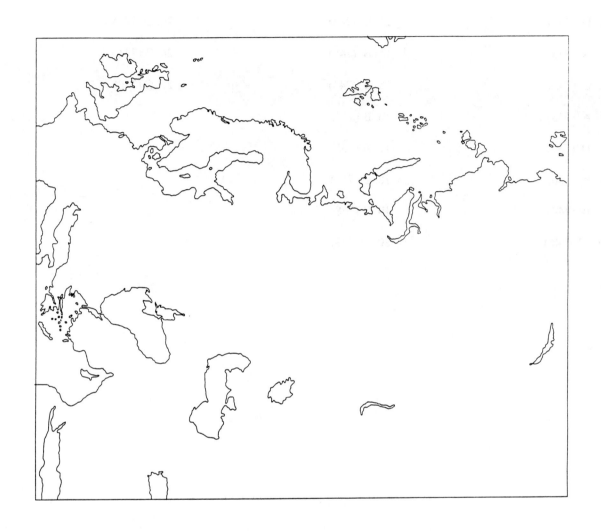

MULTIPLE CHOICE ANSWER KEY *(with page references)*

1. B (732)	11. A (740)	21. C (739)
2. C (732)	12. C (744)	22. B (739)
3. D (733)	13. D (745)	23. D (740)
4. A (733)	14. B (748)	24. B (741)
5. C (733)	15. B (744)	25. C (742)
6. A (733)	16. B (735)	
7. D (734)	17. A (736)	
8. B (736)	18. D (737)	
9. B (744)	19. B (738)	
10. C (746)	20. C (738)	

Chapter Thirty-Four
East Asia: The Recent Decades

Practice Test

1. Which of the following was among the East Asian nations that quickly switched to a market-oriented economy during the postwar era?
    - a. China
    - b. Japan
    - c. North Korea
    - d. Vietnam

2. The Supreme Allied Commander in Japan after World War II was
    - a. George Patton
    - b. George Marshall
    - c. Douglas MacArthur
    - d. Dwight Eisenhower

3. In Japan after World War II, Allied forces established a new constitution that
    - a. created a British-style parliament
    - b. denied women the right to vote
    - c. protected Japan's right to arm itself beyond self-defense
    - d. all of the above

4. The Liberal Democratic Party in 1955 was the creation of a merger of
    - a. two Socialist parties
    - b. a liberal and a conservative party
    - c. the two big conservative parties
    - d. none of the above

5. Which of the following contributed to Japanese economic growth after World War II?
    - a. cheap oil and American sponsorship in the international community
    - b. a revolution in Japanese education
    - c. the abundance of high-quality, cheap labor
    - d. all of the above

6. During the years 1991 to 1999, Japan
    - a. experienced a decline in labor costs
    - b. experienced its deepest postwar recession
    - c. implemented a stricter protectionist policy
    - d. saw a rise in employment among factory workers

7. "Brainwashing" refers to the
    - a. study and process of indoctrination
    - b. redirection of technical laborers to meet economic needs
    - c. perversion of politically correct doctrines
    - d. all of the above

8. The party chairman and head of state in postwar China was
    - a. Chao En-lai
    - b. Ho Chi Minh
    - c. Mao Zedong
    - d. Deng Xiaoping

9. The Great Leap Forward
    - a. was a great success for Mao Zedong
    - b. was an utter failure with consequent widespread hunger and malnutrition
    - c. called for a new revolution to create a truly egalitarian culture in China
    - d. emphasized ideology and not incentives

10. The Soviet Union condemned the "Great Leap Forward" as
    a. a return to capitalism
    b. a form of brainwashing
    c. "leftist fanaticism"
    d. "philosophical idealism"

11. In May 1989, the student protests in Tiananmen Square were
    a. crushed with tanks and troops
    b. supported by Deng Xiaoping
    c. resolved with help from the United States
    d. none of the above

12. During the 1990s, China's foreign relations with
    a. Russia further degenerated
    b. the United States improved
    c. Southeast Asia improved
    d. both a and b

13. The Korean War began in 1950 when
    a. North Korea invaded South Korea
    b. South Korea invaded North Korea
    c. China blockaded South Korea
    d. Douglas MacArthur invaded Panmunjom

14. The head of the Vietnamese Communist Party was
    a. Pol Pot
    b. Ho Chi Minh
    c. Chun Doo-hwan
    d. Park Chung-hee

15. In 1979, Vietnam was attacked by the
    a. Viet Minh
    b. American forces at Dien Bien Phu
    c. Communist Khmer Rouge
    d. Chinese, who wanted to absorb it

16. When Japan regained its sovereignty in April 1952
    a. Japanese culture underwent significant change
    b. Japan distanced itself from the West
    c. the changeover was hardly noticed
    d. both a and b

17. Teng's greatest achievements after 1978 was to
    a. improve relations between China and the Soviet Union
    b. demonstrate the superiority of market incentives over central planning
    c. demonstrate the superiority of central planning over market incentives
    d. improve relations between China and the U.S.

18. Under Teng
    a. the "unit" increased in importance
    b. the "unit" decreased in importance
    c. party cadres exercised more control
    d. "units" were abandoned

19. China's economic growth under Teng was fueled by
    a. cheap labor
    b. tariffs
    c. free trade
    d. both a and b

20. During the first months of the Korean War
    a. South Korean and Chinese troops pushed back UN forces
    b. U.S. troops drove deep into North Korea
    c. U.S. and South Korean troops were driven southward
    d. both a and c

21. After the Korean War
    a. South Korea quickly embraced democracy
    b. North Korea quickly embraced democracy
    c. South Korea remained a closed, authoritarian state
    d. North Korea remained a closed, authoritarian state

22. The Battle of Dien Bien Phu in 1954
    a. began the anticolonial war against the French
    b. ended the anticolonial war against the French
    c. resulted in a unified Vietnamese nation
    d. marked the beginning of U.S. involvement in Vietnam

23. With the collapse of the Soviet Union, Vietnam
    a. withdrew from Cambodia
    b. improved relations with China
    c. joined the ASEAN
    d. all of the above

24. The Khmer Rouge was led by
    a. Ho Chi Minh
    b. Ngo Dinh Diem
    c. Pol Pot
    d. Roh tae-woo

25. The engine for change in postwar Japan was
    a. occupation reforms
    b. economic growth
    c. expansion of higher education
    d. all of the above

Where

The Cold War occasionally broke out in active confrontation, as was the case with the Korean War from 1950 to 1953 and the Vietnam War from about 1965 to 1973. Study Map 34-3 (Vietnam) on page 765 of your textbook. Compare it with Map 34-2 (Korean peninsula) on page 764. How were the geopolitical arrangements of Vietnam and Korea reflective of the Cold War? Now look at Map 34-1 on page 757 of your textbook. How have the maps changed in our contemporary world? Is there still a Cold War of sorts going on with North Korea?

How and Why

1. What were the specific provisions of the constitution imposed on Japan by the Allied powers after World War II? How was Japan limited by this constitution?

2. How would you describe the "economic miracle" of Japan since 1945? What role did the United States have in this development? How did Japanese society change as a result? Why did Japan languish in recession during the 1990s?

3. Describe the Great Proletarian Cultural Revolution in China. Compare its goals with those of the Great Leap Forward. Why did these movements fail?

4. Discuss the political, social, and economic developments in China after the death of Mao in 1976. In what ways did Teng adhere to Mao's policies and how did he change them? Would you term Teng a "progressive"? What has been the general position of the Communist Party in the 1990s? What is China's current position toward Taiwan?

5. Discuss the relationship of North and South Korea. In what specific ways did their respective political and economic policies differ since the 1950s? Where do you think the future of the two countries is headed? Are there any current incentives for the Koreas to unite?

6. Why did the United States get involved in a war against Vietnam? Why ultimately did the United States lose this war and how has Vietnam fared since 1975?

Map Labeling

Study Map 34-1 on page 757 of your textbook. On the map provided for you on the next page identify the following states:

1. Pakistan
2. Singapore
3. Philippines
4. China
5. Japan
6. Indonesia
7. Taiwan
8. India
9. Nepal
10. South Korea
11. Laos
12. Myanmar
13. North Korea
14. Bangladesh
15. Cambodia
16. Sri Lanka
17. Vietnam
18. Mongolia
19. Afghanistan
20. Kazakhstan

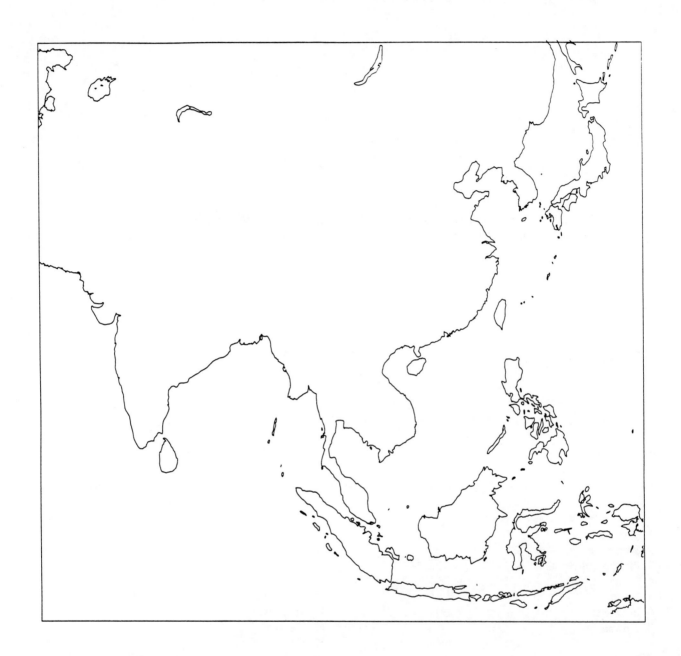

MULTIPLE CHOICE ANSWER KEY *(with page references)*

1. B (756)
2. C (756)
3. A (756)
4. C (758)
5. D (758)
6. B (759)
7. A (760)
8. C (760)
9. B (760)
10. C (761)
11. D (761)
12. C (763)
13. A (763)
14. B (765)
15. D (766)
16. C (757)
17. B (762)
18. B (762)
19. D (762)
20. C (764)
21. D (764)
22. B (764)
23. D (766)
24. C (767)
25. D (759)

Chapter Thirty-Five
The Emerging Nations of Africa, Asia, and Latin America Since 1945

Practice Test

1. In which of the following areas has decolonization notably taken place?
    a. India
    b. Pakistan
    c. Africa
    d. all of the above

2. One of the most important general trends in emerging countries is
    a. their resistance to forging new relationships with Western powers
    b. the lack of economic interdependence with established countries
    c. the fact that participatory government has gained ground
    d. both b and c

3. After the Nationalist Party came to power in 1948, South Africa was governed according to the policy of
    a. *apartheid*
    b. "enlightened democracy"
    c. *glasnost*
    d. detente

4. The African National Congress flourished under the leadership of
    a. P. W. Botha
    b. Nelson Mandela
    c. F. W. de Klerk
    d. Desmond Tutu

5. In the postwar world, the Zionist movement received a boost in acceptance because of the
    a. efforts of Theodore Herzl
    b. British Balfour Declaration
    c. need of the Allied powers to atone for the Holocaust
    d. support of Egypt after World War II

6. The refusal of the Arab states to accept the UN resolution on the creation of Israel resulted in the
    a. Suez Canal crisis
    b. occupation of the Sinai and Golan Heights by Egypt
    c. October War of 1973
    d. the Israeli-Arab War of 1948

7. The overriding problem for India has been the
    a. lack of natural resources
    b. cleft between the Hindu majority and the large Muslim minority
    c. lack of a stable political foundation
    d. disruptive radical political fringe

8. The Shah of Iran was overthrown in 1978 by the Shi'ite religious leader
    a. Saddam Hussein
    b. Ruhollah Khomeini
    c. Muhammad Reza
    d. Muhammad Ali Jinnah

9. Who of the following Indian leaders was assassinated by extremists?
    a. Mohandas Gandhi
    b. Rajiv Gandhi
    c. Indira Gandhi
    d. all of the above

10. Which of the following is an Indian problem that has yet to be solved?
    a. overpopulation
    b. poverty
    c. separatist movements
    d. all of the above

11. Liberation theology
    a. combines Christian support for the poor with Marxist ideology
    b. is based in the Catholic church and is popular among the elite classes of Latin America
    c. has tended to support the status quo political regimes of Latin America
    d. was well-focused in the 1930s but has lost its appeal in the contemporary world

12. In foreign affairs, the Cuban Revolution was characterized by a
    a. sharp break with the Soviet Union
    b. commitment to human rights throughout the world
    c. sharp break with the United States
    d. both a and b

13. The Sandinista Revolution came to an end abruptly with the
    a. assassination of Humberto Ortega
    b. fall of the Soviet Union, which had provided economic support
    c. loss of the Nicaraguan presidential election in 1990
    d. expulsion of Nicaragua from the United Nations

14. Under the leadership of Leopoldo Galtieri in 1982, the Argentinean military launched an ill-fated invasion of
    a. the Galapagos Islands   c. Paraguay
    b. the Falkland Islands   d. Uruguay

15. Representatives of Egypt and Israel reached a peace agreement in 1978/1979 when they signed the
    a. Balfour Declaration   c. Palestinian Accords
    b. Camp David Accords   d. Likud Framework

16. The difficulties and instability of the newly decolonized states stem from
    a. overpopulation
    b. lack of an educated middle class
    c. class differences
    d. all of the above

17. Nowhere is the dramatic continuity of arbitrary colonial territories and emergent independent states clearer than in
    a. Africa
    b. Latin America
    c. Southeast Asia
    d. South Asia

18. The transition from colonial to independent rule in Africa
    a. was fraught with bloody wars of liberation
    b. often resulted in tribal and regional revolts
    c. was very smooth
    d. both a and b

19. Nowhere was the aftermath of independence bloodier than in
    a. South Africa
    b. Pakistan
    c. Argentina
    d. Nigeria

20. Which was a major development in the postwar Muslim world?
    a. the creation of Israel
    b. the increase in the importance of oil
    c. the Iranian Revolution
    d. all of the above

21. Islamist movements in recent decades tend to emphasize
    a. theocracy
    b. religious pluralism
    c. social and political justice
    d. jihad against non-Muslims

22. The background of modern Islamist reform lies in
    a. European expansion since the 1400s
    b. the creation of Israel
    c. resurgent Shi'ism
    d. both b and c

23. The architect and first president of Pakistan was
    a. Mohammad Khatami
    b. Hashemi Rafsanjani
    c. Muhammad Ali Jinnah
    d. Shah Reza Pahlavi

24. Institutionally, since World War II Mexico
    a. has gone through extensive political changes
    b. has become a single party state
    c. has undergone few political changes
    d. has diversified its economy

25. The major industrial nation in Latin America is
    a. Mexico
    b. Brazil
    c. Argentina
    d. Chile

Where

Analyze Map 35-1 on page 771 of your textbook concerning the decolonization of Western powers after World War II. How extensive was the process of decolonization and what areas of the world were primarily affected?

How and Why

1. What was the result of the creation of the state of Israel in 1948? What has been the general Arab reaction to this development? What are the Camp David Accords and what impact have they had on the situation in the Middle East?

2. What are some of the major problems on the Indian subcontinent? Name some of the historic problems between India and Pakistan. Is there a possibility of unity in this region of the world?

3. What have been the major revolutionary changes in Latin America since 1945? What role did the United States and the Soviet Union play in this region? Why has there not been more revolutionary activity in Latin America?

4. Discuss the Nigerian civil war during the 1960s and 1970s. Why did it take place and how did it reflect many of the problems confronting new countries in Africa during the postcolonial period? Have these problems been resolved in Nigeria?

5. What social and economic problems has Mexico faced since World War II? Which political party remained in power until the late 1980s? Why has this apparent stability not resulted in a more productive and wealthier society?

Map Labeling

Identify the nations of the modern Middle East on Map 35-2 on page 778 of your textbook. Place the locations of these states on the map provided. Shade in the countries that have significant non-Muslim communities.

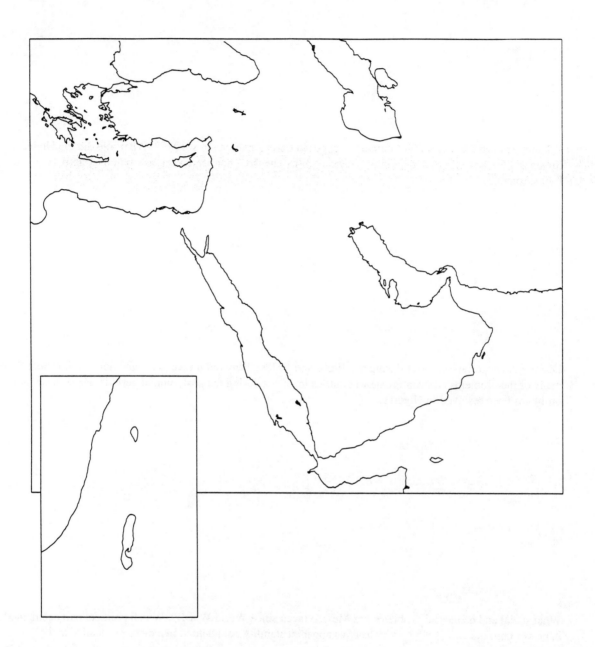

MULTIPLE CHOICE ANSWER KEY *(with page references)*

1. D (770)
2. C (770)
3. A (774)
4. B (774)
5. C (776)
6. D (776)
7. B (782)
8. B (781)
9. D (782)
10. D (782)

11. A (784)
12. C (785)
13. C (786)
14. B (786)
15. B (777)
16. D (771)
17. A (772)
18. B (772)
19. D (773)
20. D (775)

21. C (780)
22. A (780)
23. C (781)
24. C (787)
25. B (787)

LECTURE COMPANION

The following lecture note pages can be used to record your instructor's lectures and assignments for each chapter.

Chapter 15
EUROPE TO THE EARLY 1500s: REVIVAL, DECLINE, AND RENAISSANCE

Lecture Notes   **Date:**_____

Chapter 16
THE AGE OF REFORMATION AND RELIGIOUS WARS

Lecture Notes Date:_____

Chapter 17
AFRICA (ca. 1000-1800)

Lecture Notes Date:_____

Chapter 18
CONQUEST AND EXPLOITATION:
THE DEVELOPMENT OF THE TRANSATLANTIC ECONOMY

Lecture Notes   **Date:**_____

Chapter 19
EAST ASIA IN THE LATE TRADITIONAL ERA

Lecture Notes Date:_____

Chapter 20
EUROPEAN STATE BUILDING AND WORLDWIDE CONFLICT

Lecture Notes　　　　　　　　　　　　　　　　　　　　　　　　　**Date:**_____

Chapter 21
EUROPEAN SOCIETY UNDER THE OLD REGIME

Lecture Notes Date:_____

Chapter 22
THE LAST GREAT ISLAMIC EMPIRES (1500-1800)

Lecture Notes   **Date:**_____

Chapter 23
THE AGE OF EUROPEAN ENLIGHTENMENT

Lecture Notes Date:_____

Chapter 24
REVOLUTIONS IN THE TRANSATLANTIC WORLD

Lecture Notes   **Date:**_____

Chapter 25
POLITICAL CONSOLIDATION IN NINETEENTH-CENTURY EUROPE AND NORTH AMERICA, 1815-1880

Lecture Notes   Date:_____

Chapter 26
NORTHERN TRANSATLANTIC ECONOMY AND SOCIETY, 1815-1914

Lecture Notes Date:_____

Chapter 27
LATIN AMERICA: FROM INDEPENDENCE TO THE 1940S

Lecture Notes Date:_____

Chapter 28
INDIA, THE ISLAMIC HEARTLANDS, AND AFRICA:
THE ENCOUNTER WITH THE MODERN WEST (1800-1945)

Lecture Notes Date:_____

Chapter 29
MODERN EAST ASIA

Lecture Notes Date:_____

Chapter 30
IMPERIALISM AND WORLD WAR I

Lecture Notes   **Date:**_____

Chapter 31
DEPRESSION, EUROPEAN DICTATORS, AND THE AMERICAN NEW DEAL

Lecture Notes   **Date:**_____

Chapter 32
WORLD WAR II

Lecture Notes **Date:**_____

Chapter 33
THE WEST SINCE WORLD WAR II

Lecture Notes Date:_____

Chapter 34
EAST ASIA: THE RECENT DECADES

Lecture Notes Date:_____

Chapter 35
THE EMERGING NATIONS OF AFRICA, ASIA AND LATIN AMERICA SINCE 1945

Lecture Notes   **Date:**_____